CONTEMPORARY'S

EXERCISING YOUR ENGLISH

Language Skills for Developing Writers

BOOK 2

Project Editors
Betsy Rubin
Pat Fiene

CB

CONTEMPORARY BOOKS

a division of NTC/CONTEMPORARY PUBLISHING GROUP
Lincolnwood, Illinois USA

Some of the material that appears in this book
also appears in Contemporary's *GED Writing Skills
Workbook, Book 2*. Copyright © 1988 by
Contemporary Books, Inc. (ISBN: 0-8092-5813-7)

ISBN: 0-8092-4080-7

Published by Contemporary Books,
a division of NTC/Contemporary Publishing Group, Inc.,
4255 West Touhy Avenue,
Lincolnwood (Chicago), Illinois 60712-1975 U.S.A.
© 1991 by NTC/Contemporary Publishing Group, Inc.

1 2 3 4 5 6 7 8 9   C(K)   16 15 14 13 12

Editorial Director
Caren Van Slyke

Editorial
Carol Arenberg
Lisa Black
Karin Evans
Robin O'Connor

Editorial Production Manager
Norma Fioretti

Production Editor
Jean Farley Brown

Production Assistant
Marina Micari

Cover Design
Lois Koehler

Typography
Impressions, Inc.
Madison, Wisconsin

CONTENTS

TO THE LEARNER

Contemporary's *Exercising Your English: Book 2* is designed to help you develop a command of spelling, capitalization, and punctuation rules. It is one of a series of three workbooks providing extensive practice in grammar, spelling, sentence structure, and other writing skills. Your instructor may assign the workbooks in one of several ways:

    1) to supplement the grammar or writing reference book you are using in class

    2) to use as main texts to reinforce in-class instruction

    3) to use as self-study tools for help with the specific problems that appear in your writing.

Now here's a look at what you'll find in *Exercising Your English: Book 2*.

Skills Inventory

Your instructor may ask you to take the Skills Inventory test on pages 1–3 to pinpoint your strengths and weaknesses in spelling, capitalization, and punctuation. After you complete the Inventory, check your answers against those in the Answers and Explanations on pages 5–6. Then refer to the Skills Inventory Evaluation Chart on page 4 to see which exercises to emphasize as you work through this book.

Exercises

Before doing each exercise, read the brief guide at the top of the page. This will help you focus on the rules you'll need to know to complete the exercise. Be sure, also, to read and follow the directions carefully as you do the exercise. Then check your answers against the Answer Key in the back of this book. If you have made more than a few errors, review the rule, check your class reference book or perhaps a dictionary, or see your instructor for more help.

Extra Practice

Immediately following many exercises, you'll find Extra Practice exercises. These brief exercises give you the chance to apply the spelling, capitalization, or punctuation rules to your own writing. Here, you'll be able to say something about your own life or ideas. Since your answers will be your own—different from those of your classmates—no answers are provided in the back of the book.

Review Exercises

After each section is a review exercise that will help you pull together what you have just practiced. These exercises give you the chance to find out if you still need to study the area of spelling, capitalization, or punctuation covered in the section. Be sure to check your answers against the Answer Key as soon as you complete the exercise.

Final Skills Inventory

When you have finished the workbook, you can take the Final Skills Inventory on pages 53–55 to see how well you have mastered all the material you have practiced. Again, be sure to check your answers against those in the Answers and Explanations on pages 57–58. If you discover you are still having problems, use the Final Skills Inventory Evaluation Chart on page 56 to identify the specific areas you need to review.

A Word About First Impressions

Your vocabulary may be extensive, your grammar may be impeccable, and your sentences may be eloquent—but all of these abilities will be lost on the reader if your writing does not make a good *first* impression. What *do* readers notice first? Spelling, capitalization, and punctuation! Just imagine an interviewer with 100 job applications to read. She is poised and ready to throw into the garbage any application form with mechanical errors . . . but she is delighted to find one that has been carefully and correctly written. Good spelling, capitalization, and punctuation skills will impress your readers right from the start, will keep them reading what you've written, and will help them view your ideas in a positive light. They can also give you an edge in the job market, in education, and in your personal life. We hope you'll enjoy doing the exercises in *Exercising Your English: Book 2* and wish you lots of success in the future!

SKILLS INVENTORY

> **DIRECTIONS:** If a word is misspelled in the following sets of words, blacken the space in the answer grid over the number that corresponds to the misspelled word. If there is no misspelled word, blacken the space numbered (5). No set has more than one misspelled word.

Part 1   SPELLING

Example: **(1)** *spiteful* **(2)** *hateful* **(3)** *disagreeable*
(4) *troublsome*

◯ ◯ ◯ ● ◯
1 2 3 4 5

1. **(1)** eight **(2)** niece **(3)** cieling **(4)** yield

2. **(1)** amusement **(2)** replacable **(3)** combining
(4) improvement

3. **(1)** separate **(2)** favorite **(3)** benafit **(4)** estimate

4. **(1)** windowsills **(2)** treettop **(3)** payroll
(4) housewares

5. **(1)** fualt **(2)** quarrel **(3)** individual **(4)** language

6. **(1)** unopened **(2)** uneasy **(3)** unecessary
(4) unusual

7. **(1)** satisfactory **(2)** volunteer **(3)** reinforce
(4) troppical

8. **(1)** intoduction **(2)** conclusion **(3)** paragraph
(4) sentence

9. **(1)** striveing **(2)** pricing **(3)** relaying **(4)** sloppily

10. **(1)** atom **(2)** atitude **(3)** application **(4)** aptitude

11. **(1)** handbags **(2)** employees **(3)** catalogues
(4) directorys

12. **(1)** conceal **(2)** spread **(3)** unresonable
(4) heaven

13. **(1)** battlefield **(2)** either **(3)** foreign **(4)** wierd

14. **(1)** male **(2)** mail **(3)** bail **(4)** bale

15. **(1)** annoyance **(2)** happyness **(3)** penniless
(4) buyer

16. **(1)** plummer **(2)** whack **(3)** kneel **(4)** phrase

17. **(1)** chaos **(2)** approach **(3)** floating **(4)** aboard

(continued)

18. (1) belonging (2) becoming (3) begining
     (4) betraying

18. ○ ○ ○ ○ ○
     1 2 3 4 5

19. (1) perfer (2) theater (3) hundred (4) interesting

19. ○ ○ ○ ○ ○
     1 2 3 4 5

20. (1) committed (2) inhibitted (3) regretted
     (4) allotted

20. ○ ○ ○ ○ ○
     1 2 3 4 5

Part II CAPITALIZATION AND PUNCTUATION

> **DIRECTIONS:** The following sentences contain errors in capitalization
> and punctuation. If there is an error, blacken the
> numbered space in the answer grid that corresponds to
> the error. If there is no error, blacken the space
> numbered (5). No sentence contains more than one
> error.

Example: When Steve went to Safeway, he had grapes cheese, and bologna
                        1   2   3   4

on his shopping list.

○ ○ ● ○ ○
1 2 3 4 5

21. The tall childrens' parents are, surprisingly, both short.
                   1   2   3   4

21. ○ ○ ○ ○ ○
     1 2 3 4 5

22. The director said, " Are you ready"?
                    1 2 3   4

22. ○ ○ ○ ○ ○
     1 2 3 4 5

23. Warren Beatty, who is both an actor and a director, is the brother of
                  1   2   3

Actress Shirley MacLaine.
   4

23. ○ ○ ○ ○ ○
     1 2 3 4 5

24. When my brother Francis joined the United States Air Force, he was
               1   2   3   4

sixteen years old.

24. ○ ○ ○ ○ ○
     1 2 3 4 5

25. Itzak Perlman had polio as a child, however, he conquered his
                     1   2   3

affliction and became a renowned violinist.
    4

25. ○ ○ ○ ○ ○
     1 2 3 4 5

26. Here are the scores; Chicago—4, Boston—2, New York—6,
                       1   2   3

Cleveland—3.
        4

26. ○ ○ ○ ○ ○
     1 2 3 4 5

27. When Gene Kelly danced and sang "Singin' in the Rain," was he
                               1   2   3

really getting wet.
            4

27. ○ ○ ○ ○ ○
     1 2 3 4 5

(continued)

28. The Quaker Oats co. has offices in many cities, including Chicago.
   <u> </u>₁   ₂ ₃   ₄
   28. ○₁ ○₂ ○₃ ○₄ ○₅

29. "Call Uncle Norman," said my mother, "And tell him we're fine."
       ₁   ₂   ₃   ₄
   29. ○₁ ○₂ ○₃ ○₄ ○₅

30. Meet me at 5:00; otherwise, we wo'nt make it to the wedding on
             ₁ ₂   ₃   ₄
   time.
   30. ○₁ ○₂ ○₃ ○₄ ○₅

31. We'd like to visit with you; but we're due at the airport.
     ₁   ₂   ₃   ₄
   31. ○₁ ○₂ ○₃ ○₄ ○₅

32. Chico trained for the Boston Marathon by running at least, ten miles
                  ₁   ₂   ₃   ₄
   a day.
   32. ○₁ ○₂ ○₃ ○₄ ○₅

33. Chief Steward Lapinsky said, "Its time to meet the leader of our
         ₁   ₂ ₃   ₄
   union."
   33. ○₁ ○₂ ○₃ ○₄ ○₅

34. Judge Connors asked Sue Ann "if she'd like to change her plea.
                  ₁   ₂   ₃ ₄
   34. ○₁ ○₂ ○₃ ○₄ ○₅

35. The shuttle may land at White Sands, New Mexico; the Kennedy
                            ₁   ₂
   Space Center, Florida; or an undesignated spot, in the Pacific.
                  ₃   ₄
   35. ○₁ ○₂ ○₃ ○₄ ○₅

36. My greek neighbors always bring us the most delicious foods:
        ₁   ₂
   baklava, spanakopita, and dolmades.
         ₃   ₄
   36. ○₁ ○₂ ○₃ ○₄ ○₅

37. In the Western part of the state, there are many national parks.
          ₁   ₂   ₃   ₄
   37. ○₁ ○₂ ○₃ ○₄ ○₅

38. "Come right now!" shouted the paramedic to his partner. This
             ₁ ₂   ₃
   patient needs both of us."
                       ₄
   38. ○₁ ○₂ ○₃ ○₄ ○₅

39. When this year's elections take place, who do you think will have
              ₁   ₂
   more seats in Congress, the democrats or Republicans?
                 ₃   ₄
   39. ○₁ ○₂ ○₃ ○₄ ○₅

40. He told them to put it on the city's bill. "After all," he said, "Don't I
                          ₁   ₂ ₃
   deserve some benefits?"
                     ₄
   40. ○₁ ○₂ ○₃ ○₄ ○₅

Answers and Explanations begin on page 5.

4

SKILLS INVENTORY EVALUATION CHART

DIRECTIONS: After completing the Skills Inventory, check your answers by using the Skills Inventory Answers and Explanations, pages 5–6. Write the total number of *correct* answers for each skill area in the blank lines below. If you have *more than one incorrect* answer in any skill area, you need more practice. The chart shows you which workbook exercises you'll need to review.

Skill Area	Item Numbers	Total	Number Correct	Exercise Numbers
Part I Spelling	1–20	20	____	1–14
Part II Capitalization	23, 28, 29, 36, 37, 39, 40	7	____	15–24
End punctuation	27	1	____	25–26
Commas	31, 32, 35	3	____	27–30, 33
Semicolons	25	1	____	31–33, 37
Colons	26	1	____	34, 37
Apostrophes	21, 30, 33	3	____	35–37
Quotation marks	22, 34, 38	3	____	38–42

Note: Items 14, 17, and 24 are correct.

Answers and Explanations   SKILLS INVENTORY

> **DIRECTIONS:** After completing the Skills Inventory (pages 1–3), use the Answers and Explanations to check your work. *On these pages*, circle the number of each item you correctly answered. Then turn to the Skills Inventory Evaluation Chart (page 4) and follow the directions given.

Part I   SPELLING

1. (3) ceiling — The *"i* before *e* except after *c"* rule applies here.

2. (2) replaceable — When a vowel suffix is added, the silent *e* is kept if it follows *c* or *g* (unless the suffix begins with *i*).

3. (3) benefit — The unstressed vowel in this *word* is spelled with *e*, not *a*.

4. (2) treetop — This compound word is formed from the words *tree* and *top*. Therefore, there is no double letter.

5. (1) fault — The correct vowel pattern for this word is *au*. It has the same sound as the *au* combination in *August*.

6. (3) unnecessary — This word is made up of the prefix *un* plus the base word *necessary*. Therefore, the letter *n* appears twice.

7. (4) tropical — Pronouncing this word in syllables will help you remember that it contains only one *p: trop/i/cal*.

8. (1) introduction — If you pronounce the original word ("intoduction") as it is misspelled, you will hear that the letter *r* is missing. The correct spelling includes the *r*.

9. (1) striving — Usually, the silent *e* at the end of a word is dropped before a vowel suffix is added.

10. (2) attitude — Pronouncing this word in syllables may help you to remember that two *t*'s follow the *a: at/ti/tude*.

11. (4) directories — The word *directory* ends in *y* after a consonant, so the plural is correctly formed by changing *y* to *i* and adding *es*.

12. (3) unreasonable — The correct vowel pattern for this word is *ea*. It has the same sound as the *ea* combination in the word *each*.

13. (4) weird — This is an exception to the *"i* before *e* except after *c"* rule.

14. (5) No error

15. (2) happiness — In words ending in *y* after a consonant, the *y* is changed to *i* before most suffixes are added.

16. (1) plumber — *Plumber* has a silent *b*, as in *climb*.

17. (5) No error

(continued)

18. **(3)** beginning   The word *begin* ends with one vowel and one consonant, and the stress is on the final syllable. Therefore, the final consonant is doubled before a vowel suffix is added.

19. **(1)** prefer   This word is frequently mispronounced. If you pronounce it correctly ("pre/fer," not "per/fer"), you will spell it correctly.

20. **(2)** inhibited   Since the stress does not fall on the final syllable of *inhibit*, the final consonant is not doubled before *ed* is added.

Part II CAPITALIZATION AND PUNCTUATION

21. **(1)** The possessive form of *children* is *children's.*

22. **(4)** The question mark belongs inside the quotation marks because the quoted words form a question.

23. **(4)** The common noun *actress* should not be capitalized; it is not part of a title or name.

24. **(5)** No error

25. **(2)** A semicolon, not a comma, is needed before the conjunctive adverb *however.*

26. **(1)** A colon, not a semicolon, is used before a list of items.

27. **(4)** The sentence is a question and should end with a question mark.

28. **(2)** *Co.* is part of the name of the company and should be capitalized.

29. **(4)** Although *and* begins the second half of a divided quotation, it does not begin a new sentence, so it should not be capitalized.

30. **(4)** Whenever *not* is part of a contraction, the apostrophe goes in place of the missing *o: n't.* The correctly spelled contraction here is *won't.*

31. **(2)** A comma, not a semicolon, is used to separate independent clauses joined by the conjunction *but.*

32. **(4)** There is no need for a comma in the phrase *at least ten miles a day.*

33. **(3)** An apostrophe is needed in *It's,* a contraction of the words *It is.*

34. **(2)** The sentence is not a direct quotation; therefore, quotation marks should not be used.

35. **(4)** No comma should be used before the phrase *in the Pacific* since this phrase is essential to the meaning of the sentence.

36. **(1)** Words derived from geographic names should be capitalized: *Greek.*

37. **(1)** The word *western* should not be capitalized here because it is being used as an adjective to tell which part of the state is being discussed, rather than as the name of a region.

38. **(3)** Quotation marks are needed here to begin the second part of a divided quotation.

39. **(4)** Names of political parties should be capitalized: *Democrats.*

40. **(3)** Although *don't* begins the second half of a divided quotation, it does not begin a new sentence and should not be capitalized.

Exercise 1 PRONUNCIATION AND SYLLABLES I

One key to better spelling is pronunciation. When you encounter a hard-to-spell word, pronounce it syllable by syllable, so that you hear the sound made by each part of the word. Hearing the sounds will help you to spell words with problem areas, such as double letters or unstressed vowel sounds.

A syllable is a word part that is pronounced as a separate sound. Usually, there is only one vowel sound in each syllable:

day	*day*	(one syllable)
muffin	*muf/fin*	(two syllables)
location	*lo/ca/tion*	(three syllables)

If you aren't sure how to pronounce a word or divide it into syllables, check a dictionary.

DIRECTIONS: Pronounce each word syllable by syllable. As you say a syllable, write it on the blank line to the right, and put a slash mark (/) between syllables. Then cover columns 1 and 2, and write the whole word in column 3.

Example: characteristic   char/ac/ter/is/tic   characteristic

1. community   _____   _____
2. environment   _____   _____
3. liquor   _____   _____
4. athlete   _____   _____
5. institution   _____   _____
6. temperature   _____   _____
7. tomorrow   _____   _____
8. committed   _____   _____
9. different   _____   _____
10. privilege   _____   _____
11. government   _____   _____
12. jewelry   _____   _____

EXTRA PRACTICE

Make your own list of two or more words that you have trouble spelling. (Hint: Look for misspelled words in your compositions, assignments, or tests.) Divide the words on your list into syllables, and pronounce each syllable as an aid to spelling.

Answers begin on page 59.

Exercise 2   PRONUNCIATION AND SYLLABLES II

When you spell, be careful not to leave out or add extra letters and syllables. Also be on the lookout for reversed letters such as p*er*fer for p*re*fer. To check for errors like these, read the word aloud exactly as you have written it. This way, you will "hear" spelling mistakes.

> **DIRECTIONS:** In each sentence, pronounce the underlined word *as it is written.* Is it spelled correctly? If so, write "OK." If not, cross it out and write the correct spelling above. Pronounce the word correctly as you write it.

Example: Ricardo is quite ~~intelligent~~ *intelligent*.

1. The bank has three <u>convient</u> locations.
2. Howard Reeves gave an excellent <u>presentatation</u>.
3. Never use tranquilizers in <u>combation</u> with alcohol.
4. Division and <u>multiplication</u> were difficult for me when I was a child.
5. That's <u>exatly</u> how I feel too.
6. Look at that <u>unususual</u> insect crawling on your salad.
7. You are <u>resposible</u> for your own belongings.
8. That question is <u>irrevelant</u>; please stick to the point.
9. Living downtown has certain <u>avdantages</u>.
10. Can you <u>explan</u> your tardiness to the principal?
11. I will not answer any questions until my <u>lawer</u> is present.
12. My brother works in a <u>libary</u>.
13. We purchased the <u>furninture</u> on the installment plan.
14. Let's hope the football team has a more <u>successful</u> season this year.
15. Katie tries to be <u>ecomical</u> when she goes shopping.

Answers begin on page 59.

Exercise 3   PRONUNCIATION AND VOWELS

Many times, a vowel combination or its placement in a word can be confusing. Pronouncing the word can help to get the order right:

influential: *in/flu/en/tial;* quiet: *qui/et*

In some vowel combinations, the order of the vowels follows a pattern, even though the combination represents more than one sound:

ea: l*ea*ther, r*ea*l

Many times, however, you must memorize the order and placement of the vowels in a word.

DIRECTIONS: In each set of words, find the misspelled word if there is one. Blacken the space in the answer grid over the number that corresponds to the misspelled word. If there is no misspelled word, blacken the space numbered (5).

Example: (1) court (2) trout (3) giudance (4) suit

1. (1) gaiety (2) villain (3) marraige (4) waive
2. (1) gauze (2) usually (3) chaulk (4) August
3. (1) trapezoid (2) paraniod (3) bunion (4) suspension
4. (1) reaserch (2) league (3) cleanser (4) aerosol
5. (1) country (2) courage (3) coupon (4) course
6. (1) tough (2) thourough (3) through (4) though
7. (1) vauge (2) valiant (3) devaluation (4) variance
8. (1) gradually (2) mutual (3) muisician (4) bruise
9. (1) launch (2) restuarant (3) guardian (4) gauge
10. (1) beutiful (2) amateur (3) bureau (4) beauty
11. (1) miniature (2) parliament (3) straight (4) aisle
12. (1) carraige (2) campaign (3) cordial (4) explanation
13. (1) pageant (2) peseant (3) present (4) pleasant
14. (1) boardroom (2) coastal (3) woarsen (4) hoarse
15. (1) biscuit (2) buisness (3) building (4) bullet

Answers begin on page 59.

Exercise 4 THE *i* + *e* COMBINATION

Follow these rules when spelling words with the *i* + *e* combination.
The letter *i* goes before the *e* in combinations:
friend, believe
except after the letter *c* sounding like *see:*
ceiling, receipt
or when *i* + *e* sounds like *ay:*
neighbor, weigh

There are some exceptions to the "*c* rule":
science, species, ancient, conscience, conscientious, financier

There are also some exceptions to the general combination rule:
weird, height, either, neither, foreign, sovereign, forfeit, leisure, seize

> **DIRECTIONS:** In each of the following sentences, underline the incorrectly spelled *i* + *e* word. Rewrite the word on the blank, spelling it correctly. If there is no misspelled word in the sentence, write "OK" on the blank.

Example: *The chief of police gave his own* <u>neice</u> *a ticket.*   _____*niece*_____

1. Can you believe how much the nieghbor's dog weighs?   1. _____
2. What a releif to have leisure time with neither work nor family pressure interfering?   2. _____
3. We didn't percieve any errors on the receipt for the freight.   3. _____
4. No mischeif is allowed at the day camp; if they misbehave, the children must forfeit their swimming privileges.   4. _____
5. The quarterback looked down the field for a reciever.   5. _____
6. Either I have been deceived, or someone has moved a peice on the chessboard.   6. _____
7. Can you conceive of anyone so weird?   7. _____
8. Scientists' goals are to end the seiges of flu that occur in winter.   8. _____

EXTRA PRACTICE

Write one paragraph that contains all of the following words:

neighbor

believe

niece

receive

friend

Answers begin on page 59.

Exercise 5   MORE SPELLING PROBLEMS

Many words are difficult to spell because they contain one or more of the following problems:

Silent letter:

gnaw (silent *g*); *descend* (silent *c*)

Double letter:

arrangement (double *r*); *possession* (double *s*, two sets)

Internal or unstressed vowel:

separate not *seperate*

solitary not *solatary*

Nonphonetic spelling (the word isn't spelled the same way as it is pronounced):

colonel; victual

DIRECTIONS: In each set of words, find the misspelled word if there is one. Blacken the space in the answer grid over the number that corresponds to the misspelled word. If there is no misspelled word, blacken the space numbered (5).

Example: (1) minite (2) privilege (3) residence (4) engineer

1. (1) curriculum (2) currious (3) circus (4) encouraging
2. (1) ache (2) acreage (3) vacate (4) vacillate
3. (1) sympathize (2) surprise (3) pleazure (4) minimize
4. (1) irrelavant (2) separate (3) dominated (4) prevalent
5. (1) diligent (2) parallel (3) fulfillment (4) intellectual
6. (1) January (2) Wednesday (3) Febuary (4) Saturday
7. (1) delegate (2) vegatable (3) permanent (4) versatile
8. (1) psychology (2) physics (3) symmetrical (4) syringe
9. (1) malign (2) gost (3) blighted (4) gnashed
10. (1) embarrass (2) acommodate (3) academy (4) necessary
11. (1) vacuum (2) perfume (3) resume (4) asume
12. (1) catalogue (2) catagory (3) magnitude (4) marathon
13. (1) morgage (2) knapsacks (3) nimbly (4) deception
14. (1) hydrant (2) analyze (3) criticyze (4) anonymous

Exercise 6   COMPOUNDS AND PREFIXES

When two words are joined to form a **compound word**, the spelling of each separate word is kept the same; the words are simply joined together;

door + knob = doorknob; light + hearted = lighthearted

A **prefix** is a word part added to the beginning of a word. The prefix itself is not a word, but it changes the meaning of the word to which it is added. When adding prefixes to words, keep the original spelling of the base word:

re + action = reaction; un + noticed = unnoticed

DIRECTIONS: Here are two different spelling practices. In the first column, combine the words and word parts. Then write the resulting word on the blank. In the second column, write "OK" if the word is properly spelled. If it is misspelled, spell the word correctly on the blank.

Example: mis + spell = ___*misspell*___   *Example:* sunshine   ___*OK*___

1. week + end = _____   1. shortstop   _____
2. room + mate = _____   2. bookeeper   _____
3. heavy + weight = _____   3. homeowner   _____
4. bar + room = _____   4. newsstand   _____
5. share + holder = _____   5. headsstrong   _____
6. re + incarnation = _____   6. unnatural   _____
7. mis + manage = _____   7. disatisfied   _____
8. pre + register = _____   8. imaterial   _____
9. pro + rated = _____   9. remploy   _____
10. in + convenient = _____   10. disagree   _____
11. un + fold = _____   11. nontoxic   _____
12. il + legible = _____   12. innedible   _____
13. super + sonic = _____   13. postdate   _____
14. semi + monthly = _____   14. discharge   _____
15. ir + regular = _____   15. irelevant   _____

EXTRA PRACTICE

1. Make up a list of five compound words.

2. Using a dictionary for help, make a list of ten words, one with each of these prefixes:

   re, mis, pre, in, il, ir, un, non, semi, dis.

Answers begin on page 59.

Exercise 7 SUFFIXES I

A **suffix** is a word part that is added to the end of a word. Use these rules to add the *s* suffix and other suffixes that begin with consonants: *ment, ful, less, ness,* and *ly.*

1) Add the *s* suffix and other consonant suffixes directly to most words:

   play — plays, improve — improvement, careful — carefully

2) If the word ends in *y* after a consonant (not a vowel), change *y* to *i* before adding a consonant suffix:

   beauty — beautiful, merry — merriment, penny — penniless

   When *y* is changed to *i*, the *s* ending becomes *es:*

   bully, — bullies, cry — cries

3) If the word ends in *s, z, sh, ch,* or *x,* the *s* ending also becomes *es* (and is pronounced as an extra syllable):

   brush — brushes, kiss — kisses, box — boxes

   Never add *'s* to make a singular noun plural or to add a verb ending:

   WRONG: *He try's*   *Three sandwich's*

   RIGHT: *He tries*   *Three sandwiches*

Note: Some words are exceptions to the rules and must be memorized:

   true — truly, argue — argument, judge — judgment

DIRECTIONS: Here are two different spelling practices. In the first column, add the suffix to each word and write the resulting word on the blank. In the second column, write "OK" if the underlined word is correctly spelled. If it is misspelled, spell the word correctly on the blank.

Example: sandwich + s = _sandwiches_

1. annoy + s = _____

2. fine + ly = _____

3. blame + less = _____

4. attach + s = _____

5. fly + s = _____

6. crazy + ness = _____

7. pay + ment = _____

8. plenty + ful = _____

9. resist + s = _____

10. pain + ful + ly = _____

Example: full <u>emploiment</u>   _employment_

1. <u>talks</u>   _____

2. two <u>baby's</u>   _____

3. a <u>committment</u>   _____

4. yours <u>truely</u>   _____

5. scared <u>witless</u>   _____

6. french <u>fry's</u>   _____

7. an <u>arguement</u>   _____

8. six <u>tests</u>   _____

9. she <u>worry's</u>   _____

10. he <u>watchs</u>   _____

Answers begin on page 59.

Exercise 8   SUFFIXES II

The following rules apply to suffixes that begin with the vowels *a, e, and o*. Some examples of these vowel suffixes are *able, ed, er, est,* and *ous*.

4) Add vowel suffixes like these directly to most words:
play — played, wait — waiter, cavern — cavernous

5) If the word ends in silent *e*, drop the *e* before adding a suffix that begins with *a, e,* or *o*.

adore — adorable, fame — famous

However, keep the silent *e* after *c* or *g*:

courage — courageous, trace —traceable

6) In one-syllable words ending in one vowel and one consonant, double the consonant before adding a suffix that begins with *a, e,* or *o*:

wrap — wrapped, big — biggest, hug — huggable

In longer words ending in one vowel and one consonant, double the consonant *only* if the stress is on the final syllable of the base word:

submit — submitted (stress on final syllable)

visit — visited (stress on first syllable)

Note: Never double *w, y,* or *x*.

7) If the word ends in *y* after a consonant (not a vowel), change *y* to *i* before adding a suffix that begins with *a, e,* or *o*.

study — studied, carry — carrier, envy — envious

DIRECTIONS: Using rules 1–7, add the vowel suffix to each word and write the word on the blank.

Example: deplore + able = _____*deplorable*_____

1. listen + er = _____
2. try + ed = _____
3. desire + able = _____
4. trap + ed = _____
5. reveal + ed = _____
6. sleepy + er = _____
7. annoy + ance = _____
8. biodegrade + able = _____
9. sloppy + est = _____
10. expel + ed = _____
11. advantage + ous = _____
12. limit + ed = _____

Answers begin on page 59.

Exercise 9   SUFFIXES III

Some suffixes begin with the letter *i; ing, ish,* and *ize* are among the most common. These suffixes, as well as the suffix *y* follow the same rules as the other vowel suffixes with the following exceptions:

8) Always keep the letter *y* before adding a suffix that begins with *i:*

   marry — marrying, thirty — thirtyish

9) Before adding *y* or a suffix beginning with *i*, drop the silent *e*, even when it follows *c* or *g:*

   race — racy, trudge — trudging

> **DIRECTIONS:** Keeping in mind rules 1–9, look at the underlined words in each sentence. If a word is spelled correctly, write "OK" above it. If it is misspelled, cross it out and write the correction above it.

OK dropping

Example: *The baby <u>loves</u> <s>droping</s> things from her high chair.*

1. It <u>seemes</u> that Mrs. Huxtable is always <u>hurring.</u>
2. Derrick <u>wonderred</u> if he'd ever get over his <u>saddness</u>.
3. The <u>lady's</u> sat down and <u>daintyly</u> <u>siped</u> their tea.
4. Ron <u>returned</u> to work, thus <u>enableing</u> Sharon to go back to college.
5. I never <u>expected</u> to see my grandmother <u>walkking</u> down the street while <u>bouncing</u> a basketball.
6. Billy <u>play's</u> with his children's <u>toies</u> more than they do; he's <u>excitted</u> because they just got some new <u>raceing</u> <u>car's</u>.
7. Do you <u>truely</u> believe that men are less <u>likly</u> to make a <u>committment</u> than women?
8. Heather <u>sincerly</u> <u>wishes</u> to apologize for her <u>thoughtless</u> <u>remarkes</u> yesterday; her <u>unkindness</u> was not intentional.

EXTRA PRACTICE

1. Write five things that you <u>enjoy doing</u>. Use the *ing* suffix correctly.

   Example: *swimming in the ocean*

2. Write five <u>plural</u> items that you buy at the grocery store. Use the *s* ending correctly.

   Example: *three boxes of crackers*

3. Write sentences using the <u>past tense</u> of each of these verbs:

   finish, stop, purchase, plan, work, marry, happen, commit.

   Example: *John finished the exam before anyone else.*

Answers begin on page 59.

Exercise 10   SPELLING REVIEW I

> **DIRECTIONS:** In each set of words, find the misspelled word if there is one. Blacken the space in the answer grid over the number that corresponds to the misspelled word. If there is no misspelled word, blacken the space numbered (5).

Example: (1) *unattractive* (2) *unsure* (3) *unecessary* (4) *united*

1. (1) households (2) reflectively (3) driveing (4) therefore
2. (1) foundry (2) contrary (3) momentary (4) gallery
3. (1) comunity (2) comical (3) commonplace (4) commercial
4. (1) yielding (2) weighing (3) dieting (4) decieving
5. (1) suffocate (2) illustrate (3) demostrate (4) irate
6. (1) impossible (2) possess (3) tresspass (4) congress
7. (1) placement (2) squarely (3) tastey (4) ninety
8. (1) strumming (2) steaming (3) aiming (4) framing
9. (1) capatalist (2) communist (3) socialist (4) realist
10. (1) irregular (2) irrelevant (3) iritate (4) ironic
11. (1) educator (2) perpendicular (3) equater (4) tutor
12. (1) variance (2) excellence (3) defiance (4) nonsence
13. (1) portrayal (2) dutyful (3) joyous (4) swaying
14. (1) endless (2) friendship (3) cioncidence (4) really
15. (1) eveness (2) thickness (3) sadness (4) strangeness
16. (1) courageous (2) wholely (3) peaceable (4) excitement
17. (1) unnatural (2) unnoticed (3) unnending (4) undo
18. (1) physics (2) phsychology (3) psychiatrist (4) psychic
19. (1) laziness (2) storibook (3) glorified (4) daylight

Exercise 11   HOMONYMS

Homonyms are words that sound alike but have different meanings and are spelled differently:

hour, our; some, sum; right, write

When you use homonyms, be sure to write the homonym that expresses the meaning you intend.

DIRECTIONS: Underline the homonym that best completes each sentence.

Example: Don't (stare, stair) at the staggering drunk!

1. Have you decided (weather, whether) you will go or not?
2. The (scene, seen) from the mountaintop is spectacular.
3. You must (great, grate) the potatoes to make hash browns.
4. The teacher will (counsel, council) all students with low grades.
5. Yesterday, the Keystones left (their, there) children at (their, they're) friend's house.
6. Each sentence should begin with a (capitol, capital) letter.
7. The tables and chairs at McDonald's are (stationery, stationary).
8. Why can't lawyers speak (plane, plain) English?
9. The (mail, male) seems to bring only bills!
10. (Your, You're) tax return is ready to be signed.
11. The (principle, principal) of the strike was to gain benefits for (principle, principal) actors and other members of the Screen Actors' Guild.
12. (Steal, Steel) is one of the strongest metals.
13. Jessica should (of, have) called sooner.
14. Eva can't (hear, here) what (your, you're) saying.
15. Clean the windows and mirrors (to, two, too).

EXTRA PRACTICE

Use each of the following words in a sentence.

their

you're

too

principle

hear

steel

You may write a separate sentence for each word or use more than one word in the same sentence.

Answers begin on page 60.

18

Exercise 12   WORDS OFTEN CONFUSED

Certain words are commonly confused because their spellings are similar:

advise (a verb meaning "to counsel")

advice (a noun meaning "a suggestion")

To select the right word, think carefully about the sentence's meaning:

I advised her to follow my *advice.*

If you are unsure about which word is correct, look up the choices in a dictionary.

DIRECTIONS: Underline the correct word choice in each of the following sentences.

Example: *It was so cold that we could see our (breath, breathe).*

1. Janice gave her room a (thorough, through) cleaning.
2. Father McGuire gives helpful (advice, advise).
3. Please try not to (loose, lose) your homework again.
4. (Where, Were) did you go last night?
5. The experimental drug may (effect, affect) your digestion.
6. He was not (conscience, conscious) of his annoying habit.
7. The directions will tell you how to (proceed, precede).
8. We had eight hours to (accept, except) or reject the offer.
9. For (desert, dessert) there is rice pudding.
10. If you have a question about benefits, contact the (personal, personnel) office.
11. All of the states have tough penalties for the use or sale of (elicit, illicit) drugs.
12. The Griffins wore their best (cloths, clothes) to their son's graduation.
13. You should (bath, bathe) an infant in lukewarm water.

EXTRA PRACTICE

Write sentences using the following words correctly.

advise   quite

clothes   than

loose   personal

You may write a separate sentence for each word or use more than one word in the same sentence. (Check your dictionary if necessary.)

Answers begin on page 60.

Exercise 13   SPELLING REVIEW II

DIRECTIONS: In each set of words, find the misspelled word if there is one. Then blacken the space in the answer grid over the number that corresponds to the misspelled word. If there is no misspelled word, blacken the space numbered (5).

Example: (1) *peirce* (2) *conceive* (3) *believe* (4) *seizure*

1. (1) textbook (2) bilboard (3) update (4) teacup
2. (1) maxamum (2) minimum (3) premium (4) forum
3. (1) seen (2) redeem (3) extreem (4) theme
4. (1) surgury (2) perjury (3) luxury (4) treasury
5. (1) chastity (2) sanity (3) specialty (4) continueity
6. (1) follow (2) below (3) solo (4) mellow
7. (1) appealling (2) retelling (3) sailing (4) distilling
8. (1) immature (2) import (3) imperial (4) immobile
9. (1) baitted (2) batted (3) hated (4) waited
10. (1) lively (2) lovable (3) valueable (4) agreeable
11. (1) frying (2) fried (3) fries (4) refried
12. (1) hurrying (2) marrying (3) worrysome (4) trying
13. (1) dissect (2) dissaster (3) dissolve (4) diseased
14. (1) affair (2) affraid (3) affected (4) affirmed
15. (1) rooftop (2) sweetheart (3) taxpayer (4) limesstone
16. (1) handfull (2) fulfill (3) refill (4) careful
17. (1) ciggarette (2) pennant (3) personnel (4) luggage
18. (1) cocktail (2) coconut (3) cocaine (4) cocoon
19. (1) grievience (2) inconvenience (3) patience (4) ingredients
20. (1) enforcement (2) arguement (3) enrichment (4) involvement

Answers begin on page 60.

Exercise 14   SPELLING REVIEW III

> **DIRECTIONS:** Check each sentence for spelling errors. If a word is misspelled, cross it out and write the correct spelling above the word. (There is no more than one misspelled word per sentence.) If all words in a sentence are spelled correctly, write "OK."

Example: Sondra said, "That teacher is ~~wierd~~ weird."

1. The post office is inconviently located.

2. I haven't recieved any explanation yet for their peculiar behavior.

3. Lorraine and her unfaithful husband have recently separated.

4. After the boy's tragic death, a child phychologist spoke to his grieving classmates.

5. It is both ilegal and immoral to sell alcohol to a minor.

6. I would have prefered to have stayed home and relax, but Gary dragged me to the miniature golf course.

7. It is finacially unwise to invest all your earnings in lottery tickets.

8. The demonstrators protested noisyly against the proposed incinerator project.

9. I hope your not going to suggest another tedious game of Go Fish.

10. Were in the world are you planning to go dressed in that bizarre outfit?

11. The outdoor wedding was a joyous occasion for all who attended.

12. Meryl begged off early, saying, "I have to get my beuty sleep."

13. My roomate is one of the most intelligent people I know, but her messages to me are full of misspellings.

14. His parents tried to sheild him from the bad influences in his neighborhood.

15. The letter was written on perfumed stationary; reading it gave me a severe headache.

Answers begin on page 60.

Exercise 15 CAPITALIZATION RULES 1–4

Use the following rules to capitalize words correctly.

1) Capitalize the pronoun *I:*

   When *I* earn my diploma, *I*'ll look for a job.

2) Capitalize the first word of a sentence:

   That news show is good. *There* should be more like it.

3) Capitalize people's names:

   Michael Jordan, Debra Sue Kowalski

4) Capitalize job and family titles when they immediately precede a person's name and are considered to be part of the name:

   Senator Jones and *Aunt* Sarah were high school sweethearts.

   Also capitalize job and family titles when they take the place of a person's name. (If a name could be inserted in place of the title, it is taking the place of a person's name):

   "Come quickly, *Nurse*," cried the *doctor.*

   (A name could be inserted in place of *Nurse* but not *doctor.*)

> **DIRECTIONS:** Check each of the following sentences for capitalization errors. If there is an error, circle the word and write it correctly above. If there is no error, write "OK."

Example: The author of the book is Alice Walker. (she) is one of my favorite writers.   *She*

1. Is Doctor Cotter a child Psychologist?

2. When Congressman Yates arrives, tell him that ms. Bain called.

3. Why have I got so many bills to pay? I owe money to my dentist, my lawyer, and my landlord.

4. Your aunt, Uncle, and Grandpa Joe are here.

5. Why is it that when i'm working there's never enough time to visit my grandmother? Perhaps I should learn to schedule my time better.

6. A Doctor spoke to Mayor Daley and Cardinal Bernardin about the local infant mortality rate.

7. Let's go to Mary Lou's! her husband works the late shift tonight, so she may be lonely.

Answers begin on page 60.

Exercise 16 CAPITALIZATION RULES 5–8

5) Capitalize geographic names and most words derived from them:

People's Republic of *China*, *Chinese* chef

Some words derived from geographic names are not capitalized:

turkish towel, *roman* numeral, *manila* envelope

Check a dictionary if you are unsure whether to capitalize a word.

6) Capitalize the names of streets, parts of town, and regions of the country:

Martin Luther King Drive, the *West Side*, the *Southwest*

Do not capitalize *north*, *south*, *east*, and *west* when used as directions:

The car was headed *west*.

7) Capitalize the names of important buildings and structures:

the *Lincoln Memorial*, the *Empire State Building*

8) Capitalize the names of historic events and periods:

World War I, the *Middle Ages*

DIRECTIONS: Check the sentences below for capitalization errors. Put three underscores under any letter that should be capitalized.

Example: *The john hancock building is on chicago's lakefront.*

1. Does aunt barbara still live in las vegas, nevada?
2. thomas jefferson lived at monticello, his home in virginia.
3. I grew up in the midwest but went to college in the east.
4. My friend darius, the crazy new yorker, lives in manhattan near the george washington bridge.
5. Anita, a professor at the university of georgia in athens, says many northerners go to school in the south.
6. in san francisco, I took a cable car to post street.
7. Whenever cousin edward eats italian food, he recalls the days he spent in milan, italy, during world war II.

EXTRA PRACTICE

Write each of the following, using capital letters correctly:

1. the name of your city or town and your state
2. your favorite ethnic food, such as *Japanese* food
3. the name of an important building in your city or town

Answers begin on page 60.

Exercise 17 CAPITALIZATION RULES 9–12

9) Capitalize the brand names of products:

   Puffs tissues, *Sanka*

10) Capitalize the names of companies, stores, banks, etc.:

   the *Shell Oil Company*, the *First National Bank*

11) Capitalize the names of specific organizations:

   the *American Heart Association*

12) Capitalize the names of political parties:

   Democrats, the *Citizens' Community Party*

DIRECTIONS: Check the following sentences for capitalization errors. Put three underscores under any letter that should be capitalized.

Example: *The coca cola company distributes sprite.*

1. The republicans have many wealthy supporters in large companies such as the xerox corporation.

2. The democrats gained seats in the House, while the republicans gained seats in the Senate.

3. The main offices of the united steel workers are in Pittsburgh.

4. To lose weight, Julie took dexatrim and joined weight watchers.

5. Call the better business bureau, and see if the charitable organization is registered.

6. Anita is active in the girl scouts of america.

7. My favorite snack, chee•tos, is made by frito-lay, inc., whose national headquarters are in Dallas.

EXTRA PRACTICE

Write each of the following, using capital letters correctly:

1. the brand name of the shampoo you use

2. the name of a store in your city

3. the name of your governor's political party

Answers begin on page 61.

Exercise 18   CAPITALIZATION RULES 13–16

13) In general, capitalize specific names but not general names:

high school, *Worcester East High School;* taxi service, *American Taxi Service*

14) Capitalize names of specific school courses but not of a general subject area unless it is a language:

algebra, *Algebra I;* auto mechanics, *Auto Mechanics 29B;* English, *English Literature 102*

15) Capitalize the names of languages, religions, and religious denominations:

Italian, Spanish, Judaism, Baptist

16) Capitalize all names referring to God, a deity, or a worshipped figure:

Christ, Allah, Krishna

DIRECTIONS: Check the following sentences for capitalization errors. Put three underscores under any letter that should be capitalized.

Example: *After graduating from high school, I attended parker college.*

1. would a presbyterian view religious holidays differently from a catholic?

2. if you took high school math, you should be ready for mathematics 101 in college.

3. uncle carl and aunt helga are close friends with professor rappaport, who teaches russian at a community college in my state.

4. the auto mechanic at midas told me he had learned his trade at the andrew jackson vocational school.

5. cynthia is studying computer science at the national institute of technology.

6. dr. mustafa azawi is an expert on islamic law and the koran.

7. if you join the jazz band, you'll get credit for music appreciation 201.

8. my favorite class is called latin american literature in the twentieth century; it is taught by a professor from columbia. we read the books in spanish, but classes are conducted in english.

9. the rabbi spoke of god and read in hebrew from the torah.

10. my uncle in korea took me to several buddhist temples.

Answers begin on page 61.

Exercise 19   CAPITALIZATION 1–16 REVIEW

> **DIRECTIONS:** Check each of the following sentences for capitalization errors. If there is a mistake, blacken the space over the number corresponding to it in the answer grid. If there is no error, blacken the space numbered (5)

Example: I prefer Doctor Stein to the Doctor that my father sees.
            1   2   3   4   ○ ○ ● ○ ○ (1 2 3 4 5)

1. Does American Airlines fly to Hawaii? I would like to visit several Islands there. [1 2 3 4] ○○○○○ 1 2 3 4 5

2. We visited the Sistine chapel in the Vatican when we were in Italy. ○○○○○ 1 2 3 4 5

3. The Gibson company donated an exquisite collection of Nigerian art to the city's largest museum. ○○○○○ 1 2 3 4 5

4. During the great Depression, President Franklin Roosevelt instituted government programs to help the unemployed. ○○○○○ 1 2 3 4 5

5. The Mississippi River is the longest River in the country. ○○○○○ 1 2 3 4 5

6. In 1988, United States citizens elected a Republican president but a largely democratic Congress. ○○○○○ 1 2 3 4 5

7. Drive South on the Indiana Tollway to East Oak Avenue. ○○○○○ 1 2 3 4 5

8. A Mother does not always win full custody of her child, especially if the father impresses a judge with his eagerness to be the custodial parent. ○○○○○ 1 2 3 4 5

9. During the Revolutionary War, the colonists fought the British with some aid from the french. ○○○○○ 1 2 3 4 5

10. The Spot Welding I Class meets in the vocational building on Lennox Avenue. ○○○○○ 1 2 3 4 5

(continued)

11. The American Cancer Society recommends the use of
$\overline{1}$ $\overline{2}$ $\overline{3}$
margarine rather than butter, so I always buy Parkay.
$\overline{4}$

11. ◯ ◯ ◯ ◯ ◯
   1 2 3 4 5

12. I use Contadina tomato products to make my italian
$\overline{1}$ $\overline{2}$ $\overline{3}$ $\overline{4}$
specialties.

12. ◯ ◯ ◯ ◯ ◯
   1 2 3 4 5

13. Dad, you can't imagine how glad i'll be to pass my Algebra
$\overline{1}$ $\overline{2}$ $\overline{3}$
203 exam.
$\overline{4}$

13. ◯ ◯ ◯ ◯ ◯
   1 2 3 4 5

14. Does ambassador Wilson really speak Swahili, German,
$\overline{1}$ $\overline{2}$ $\overline{3}$
and Chinese?
$\overline{4}$

14. ◯ ◯ ◯ ◯ ◯
   1 2 3 4 5

15. When Sister Margaret leads the children in prayer, She
$\overline{1}$ $\overline{2}$ $\overline{3}$
tells them that God loves them all.
$\overline{4}$

15. ◯ ◯ ◯ ◯ ◯
   1 2 3 4 5

16. Did you know that Reno, Nevada, is West of Los Angeles,
$\overline{1}$ $\overline{2}$ $\overline{3}$ $\overline{4}$
California?

16. ◯ ◯ ◯ ◯ ◯
   1 2 3 4 5

17. Are american compact cars costlier than the foreign
$\overline{1}$ $\overline{2}$
models, such as Volkswagens and Fiats?
$\overline{3}$ $\overline{4}$

17. ◯ ◯ ◯ ◯ ◯
   1 2 3 4 5

18. Soviet Foreign Minister Shevardnadze met with James
$\overline{1}$ $\overline{2}$
Baker, our secretary of State, to discuss deployment of
$\overline{3}$ $\overline{4}$
nuclear missiles.

18. ◯ ◯ ◯ ◯ ◯
   1 2 3 4 5

19. Most residents of Salt Lake city practice the Mormon
$\overline{1}$ $\overline{2}$ $\overline{3}$
religion, as it is commonly known.
$\overline{4}$

19. ◯ ◯ ◯ ◯ ◯
   1 2 3 4 5

20. The doctor's office is on the Northeast corner of Division
$\overline{1}$ $\overline{2}$ $\overline{3}$
and Clark Streets.
$\overline{4}$

20. ◯ ◯ ◯ ◯ ◯
   1 2 3 4 5

EXTRA PRACTICE

Write a short paragraph about someone you know. Tell where this person lives and works and what kind of car the person owns or would like to own. If you wish, tell what political party the person usually votes for and what religion he or she practices.

IMPORTANT: Include all necessary capital letters.

Answers begin on page 62.

Exercise 20 CAPITALIZATION RULES 17 AND 18

17) Capitalize abbreviated titles after a name:

John Marks, *Sr.*; William James, *Ph.D.*

Note: The first letter in the abbreviation is capitalized, as well as each letter immediately following a period.

18) Capitalize the first and last words in titles and all the important words in between:

The Grapes of *Wrath; One* from the *Heart*

Note: Words like *a, an, the, of, and, from,* and *to* are not capitalized unless they are the first or last word in a title.

DIRECTIONS: Write each sentence below on the blank that follows it. Insert capital letters as needed, using rules 1–18.

Example: *well, maestro, did you enjoy beethoven's fifth symphony?*

Well, Maestro, did you enjoy Beethoven's Fifth Symphony?

1. did you see *a nightmare on elm street* when it first came out?

_____

2. we sang "we shall overcome" in memory of dr. martin luther king, jr.

_____

3. the book *a night to remember* is about the sinking of the titanic.

_____

4. my cousin, al morales, m.d., referred me to you, doctor.

_____

5. my favorite mystery by p.d. james is *a taste for death.*

_____

6. last night we watched *from here to eternity,* a movie about world war II.

_____

7. when the concorde takes off for europe, general stone, u.s.a.f., will be aboard.

_____

8. *west side story* is loosely based on shakespeare's *romeo and juliet.*

_____

EXTRA PRACTICE

Using capital letters correctly, write the title of your favorite movie, book, and song.

Answers begin on page 62.

Exercise 21   CAPITALIZATION RULES 19–22

19) Capitalize the names of holidays:

Columbus Day, the *Fourth* of *July*

20) Capitalize the names of the days of the week:

Sunday, Wednesday

21) Capitalize the names of the months:

September, May

Do not capitalize the seasons of the year:

fall, winter, spring, summer

22) Capitalize the abbreviations *B.C.* and *A.D.*

DIRECTIONS: Check the sentences below for capitalization errors. Put three underscores under any letter that should be capitalized.

Example: is labor day always the first monday in september?

1. our anniversary, may 28, sometimes falls on memorial day.

2. macy's is open late on monday and thursday evenings.

3. florists always look forward to February 14, valentine's day.

4. we always celebrate thanksgiving on the fourth thursday in november.

5. the coins are believed to date back to somewhere between 50 b.c. and 100 a.d.

6. the office will be closed thursday and friday because we must take the monthly inventory.

7. every thirty days, more or less, we begin a new month.

8. i can never remember if halloween is on october 30 or october 31.

9. the months that have thirty days are september, april, june, and november.

10. the employees want to take the holiday on monday or friday, which would extend their weekend to three days.

Answers begin on page 62.

Exercise 22   CAPITALIZATION RULE 23

23) In a letter, capitalize each word of the opening greeting except *and:*

Dear Mr. and *Mrs. Michaels*

Capitalize the first word of the closing:

Your devoted fan; *Sincerely* yours

DIRECTIONS: Check the letter below for capitalization errors. Put three underscores under any letter that should be capitalized.

---

february 6, 1991

Mr. Jacob hargreaves
Perfect cookbooks, inc.
1946 Elm ave.
Chicago, Illinois 60600

Dear mr. Hargreaves:

In november, i ordered a set of your cookbooks, which i had seen advertised in *ladies' home journal.* it is now february, and i have not received any of the books. I couldn't even use the recipes i especially wanted for christmas cookies and fruit cake!

if you cannot guarantee that i'll have the books in six weeks—no later than march 15—please return my check. I hope to use the easter cake decorating tips i read about, so i must have the books next month.

sincerely,
estelle Louis
Howe Park Bake shoppe

Answers begin on page 62.

Exercise 23 CAPITALIZATION RULE 24

A **direct quotation** uses quotation marks ("...") to identify the speaker's exact words or thoughts.

24) Capitalize the first word in a direct quotation:

"It's time to go," explained Malcolm.

As she sat down, she thought, "*It's* great to be alive."

If a direct quotation is interrupted or divided, the second part of the quotation begins with a capital letter when a new sentence starts:

"Don't worry," said the lawyer. "*We* have plenty of solid evidence."

"Yesterday," explained the utility representative, "*was* when the payment was due."

Notice that *was* does not begin a new sentence, so it does not need to be capitalized.

DIRECTIONS: All capitalization has been omitted in the following story. Put three underscores under any letter that should be capitalized.

---

stephen smith lay in bed at monroe hospital, his mother by his side. "my son," wept mrs. smith, "was shot for wearing the wrong thing, and that's all."

on wednesday, june 10, mr. smith was shot while waiting for a bus on oak street near harbor drive. he was wearing a purple scarf with his blue windbreaker. "i didn't realize," he said later, "that those were the colors of the majestic knights or that i was on the turf of the green demons."

a passerby, jacklyn michaels, told the *daily news,* "as the attackers drove off, i saw them making gang signals." ms. michaels, a medical student at leland university, immediately shouted for help and began first aid. chong dae park, a korean immigrant who had arrived in the city only the previous saturday, heard her cries and called 911 from a nearby pay phone. "please send help!" he told the dispatcher. "a man is shot near burger king on oak street."

mr. park and ms. michaels later joined stephen's mother at the hospital, where the doctor made an announcement. "i have good news," said dr. vega. "this young man will be home in time to celebrate independence day with his family on july 4!"

Answers begin on page 63.

Exercise 24   CAPITALIZATION 1–24 REVIEW

> **DIRECTIONS:** Check each of the following sentences for capitalization errors. If there is a mistake, blacken the space over the number corresponding to it in the answer grid. If there is no error, blacken the space numbered (5).

Example: *After one <u>week's</u> vacation in <u>June</u>, <u>I</u> am really ready to enjoy the <u>Summer</u>.*
(1) (2) (3) ● (4) ... 1 2 3 4 5 (answer 4)

1. President Bush was asked by <u>general</u> <u>McComb</u> if <u>he'd</u> enjoyed his flight on the <u>Concorde</u>.
   ○ ○ ○ ○ ○   1 2 3 4 5

2. The classic horror film <u>*The*</u> *Phantom <u>of</u> <u>the</u> <u>Opera</u>* is still popular.
   ○ ○ ○ ○ ○   1 2 3 4 5

3. "<u>You</u> must move your car," <u>warned</u> the <u>officer</u>, "<u>Or</u> it will be towed away."
   ○ ○ ○ ○ ○   1 2 3 4 5

4. The <u>winter</u> <u>months</u>, especially <u>January</u>, are often depressing to people who live in the <u>midwest</u>.
   ○ ○ ○ ○ ○   1 2 3 4 5

5. Is it legal for a United States <u>Senator</u> to be the <u>spokesperson</u> for a <u>European</u> <u>company</u>?
   ○ ○ ○ ○ ○   1 2 3 4 5

6. "Is <u>Geritol</u> considered a <u>vitamin</u>?" asked Dawn. Bob replied, "<u>no</u>, it's a mixture of vitamins and minerals."
   ○ ○ ○ ○ ○   1 2 3 4 5

7. Getting up her courage, <u>Yolanda</u> said, "<u>Well</u>, <u>Doctor</u>, perhaps I should see another <u>Doctor</u> for a second opinion."
   ○ ○ ○ ○ ○   1 2 3 4 5

8. Although she has lived in this <u>country</u> most of her life, <u>Mrs.</u> Tesich still speaks only <u>Serbian</u>, the language of her native <u>Yugoslavia</u>.
   ○ ○ ○ ○ ○   1 2 3 4 5

9. The <u>Principal</u> asked <u>if</u> we would like to meet <u>Ms.</u> Johnson, his <u>assistant</u>.
   ○ ○ ○ ○ ○   1 2 3 4 5

(continued)

10. "Stop working now," ordered the monitor. "Your time on
    the Science section was up at 11:00 a.m."
    <u>1</u> ... <u>2</u> ... <u>3</u> <u>4</u>

    10. ○ ○ ○ ○ ○
         1 2 3 4 5

11. "Wait a minute!" Shouted the student. "Let me have time
    <u>1</u> ... <u>2</u> ... <u>3</u>
    to mark one last answer. Okay?"
    <u>4</u>

    11. ○ ○ ○ ○ ○
         1 2 3 4 5

12. On the West coast, Japanese cars, such as Nissans, may
    <u>1</u> <u>2</u> <u>3</u>
    be less expensive than in the East.
    <u>4</u>

    12. ○ ○ ○ ○ ○
         1 2 3 4 5

13. We saw the Spike Lee movie *Do The Right Thing* at our
    <u>1</u> <u>2</u>
    neighborhood theater.
    <u>3</u> <u>4</u>

    13. ○ ○ ○ ○ ○
         1 2 3 4 5

14. The United Auto Workers asked General Motors
    Corporation to reopen the Winter contract negotiations in
    <u>1</u> <u>2</u> <u>3</u>
    the Midwest.
    <u>4</u>

    14. ○ ○ ○ ○ ○
         1 2 3 4 5

15. "Learn your Math now," warned the high school teacher,
    <u>1</u> <u>2</u> <u>3</u>
    "or you will never make it in Basic Accounting I at
    <u>4</u>
    college."

    15. ○ ○ ○ ○ ○
         1 2 3 4 5

16. "Becoming a geologist is very important to Serena, my
    <u>1</u>
    Niece," explained Aunt Reyna, "so she'll be moving to
    <u>2</u> <u>3</u>
    the Southwest in a few weeks."
    <u>4</u>

    16. ○ ○ ○ ○ ○
         1 2 3 4 5

17. "On a closely related issue," began Speaker of the House
    <u>1</u> <u>2</u>
    Tom Foley, "The bill regarding child care is now up for
    <u>3</u> <u>4</u>
    discussion."

    17. ○ ○ ○ ○ ○
         1 2 3 4 5

18. Seven-Up, a soft drink, is owned by the Philip Morris
    <u>1</u>
    Company, a large tobacco Company.
    <u>2</u> <u>3</u> <u>4</u>

    18. ○ ○ ○ ○ ○
         1 2 3 4 5

19. My best friend Delia, who lives in the northwestern part
    <u>1</u> <u>2</u>
    of our continent, believes that clean, moist air is what
    <u>3</u>
    keeps her so healthy. don't you agree?
    <u>4</u>

    19. ○ ○ ○ ○ ○
         1 2 3 4 5

20. As the Worshippers neared Mecca, they began to give
    <u>1</u> <u>2</u>
    thanks to Mohammed with a prayer from the Koran.
    <u>3</u> <u>4</u>

    20. ○ ○ ○ ○ ○
         1 2 3 4 5

Answers begin on page 63.

Exercise 25 THE PERIOD

Use the period in these ways:

1) At the end of a sentence

   The office closes at noon on Saturdays.

2) At the end of abbreviations

   Oct.   *Mr.* Delaney   Michigan *Ave.*

   Note: Use only one period to end a sentence.

   The directions said to turn left on Carson *St.*

3) As a decimal point

   1.5 litre engine

4) Between dollars and cents

   $89.95

DIRECTIONS: Insert periods where needed in each sentence that
follows.

Example: When Ms. Wolf speaks, everyone listens

1. Dr Williams charges $4800 for an office visit
2. Mark your calendar for Fri, Mar 12th
3. The school is almost two miles (17 to be exact) from our home on W Hampshire St
4. This station sells gas for $175 a gallon I need 188 gallons to fill my empty tank
5. Rev Caldwell's notes read: "I worked on this sermon from Mon to Fri"
6. Acme Printing, Inc, is located on Seventh St near the US Post Office
7. The baby, named Joseph Cole, Jr, weighed 7 lbs, 3 oz, at birth
8. As Mr and Mrs Fareed entered, everyone became quiet
9. On the receipt he wrote, "$12 recd, full amt pd"
10. Carpeting is $1095 per sq yd The rm is 10 ft by 12 ft, so we need 120 sq ft

Answers begin on page 64.

Exercise 26 EXCLAMATION POINT AND QUESTION MARK

Use the exclamation point to indicate strong emotion:

"Good grief!" Sara shouted.

Use the question mark to end a question:

Do you have the correct time?

Joel asked, "Where is the pharmacy?"

Be careful, though. The following sentence is not a question:

Joel asked if I knew where the pharmacy was.

The sentence only states that a question was asked; therefore, it doesn't end with a question mark.

DIRECTIONS: For each sentence below, insert periods, exclamation points, and question marks where needed. You will learn more about punctuation in quotations in later lessons. In this exercise, put any end punctuation inside the quotation marks.

Example: "Aren't you ready yet?" asked Ronald.

1. "I won" exclaimed Georgianna
2. The fireman asked, "Do you have a smoke alarm"
3. "Stop, thief " shouted the enraged shopkeeper
4. Frank wondered when the babysitter would show up
5. How much rain has fallen in the past hour
6. "Get out of the apartment " ordered the tenant
7. The instructor asked how many people had taken the test before
8. "What a hoax" sputtered the swindled investors
9. Don't bananas contain a lot of potassium
10. Where can the children be I am so worried about them
11. "A question we should ask ourselves before bringing a pet into the home," began the talk show host, "is whether we truly will commit ourselves to providing for its welfare"
12. Is there an emergency exit Let's ask the landlord
13. Good heavens Did you expect a surprise party
14. Would you please get it right this time I've retyped this letter six times so far
15. If all twenty of us contribute ten dollars to the pot, we will have $20000 for the office party

Answers begin on page 64.

Exercise 27 THE COMMA I

Use the comma in these ways:

1) To separate more than two similar items in a series.

   Tomas is a *bright, cheery, fun-loving* person.

2) To set off the name or title of a person being addressed.

   Paul, I appreciate your help.

   Did you know, *Ms. Wallace,* that your bill is past due?

   The meeting has been canceled, *Mr. President.*

3) To set off a day from a year.

   The store opened on *March 3, 1975.*

   We will meet on *June 1, 1990,* at 3 P.M.

4) To set off a city or a town from a state or a country.

   I was born in *Phoenix, Arizona.*

   We met in *London, England,* in 1987.

5) To separate digits into groups of thousands.

   19,346   1,381,076

DIRECTIONS: Insert commas where needed in each sentence below. If commas are not needed, write "OK" in front of the sentence.

Example: He enjoys fishing, swimming, and water skiing.

1. Be sure all the dishes glasses and pans are clean.
2. The population of the United States in 1980 was 226504825.
3. We have offices in Los Angeles California and Dallas Texas.
4. John we need to get 15000 more signatures on the petition by October 10 1991.
5. Alesandro speaks Portuguese Spanish and English.
6. Soft drinks and snacks are included in the cost Miss Wyzinski.
7. The breakfast special consists of bacon and eggs orange or tomato juice and freshly baked muffins.
8. Do you want to visit Shana and Patrick or Gwen and James over the holiday season?
9. Thank you Professor for your help and support.
10. July 4 1776 is a significant date in the history of the United States.

Answers begin on page 64.

Exercise 28   THE COMMA II

Also put a comma:

6) Before a coordinating conjunction (*and, but, or, so, yet*) joining complete sentences:

We went to the new restaurant, *and* we had a delicious meal.

Note: Do not put a comma before a coordinating conjunction that is joining compound verbs or other compound sentence parts:

We went to the new restaurant *and* had a delicious meal.

7) After an introductory word, phrase, or clause when the rest of the sentence could stand alone as a complete thought.

Compare the two groups of examples below.

Punctuated:

Unfortunately, I will not be able to attend the party.

Near the end of the book, I lost interest in the plot.

To do well on the exam, you will have to study.

If you have any questions, please call me.

Not Punctuated:

Near the end of the book is a glossary of terms.

To do well on the exam is my goal.

DIRECTIONS: Insert commas where needed in each sentence below. If commas are not needed, write "OK" in front of the sentence.

Example: As we approached the house, the light went on.

1. While driving to San Antonio Luis and Carmen saw three dead jackrabbits at the side of the road.
2. Licking the stamps put a bad taste in my mouth.
3. He packed his bags and he put them in the back seat of his Chevy pickup.
4. I bought the suit on sale but I had to pay full price for the shoes.
5. We will meet you at the airport and drive you to your hotel.
6. Frankly I did not enjoy the movie very much.
7. When you go to the store please buy me a gallon of milk.
8. We must learn to work together as a team or we will fail.

Answers begin on page 64.

Exercise 29   THE COMMA III

Also use the comma in these ways:

8) To set off a word, phrase, or clause that gives additional but nonessential information.

I will, *unfortunately,* be out of town on that date.

Ms. Weber, *the boss,* is a real tyrant.

Lu, *who lives down the hall,* has just painted the apartment.

I would like you to meet Marie, *my sister.*

9) To set off contrasting expressions.

The bigger they are, *the harder they fall.*

The eggs are served with pancakes, *rather than toast.*

Barbara, *not her brother,* shoveled the walk.

10) To set off a speaker's name from a quotation of his or her words.

Bertha asked, "Why didn't you call?"

"A penny," *said Zeke,* "is not worth saving anymore."

"My shoes are killing me," *moaned Ronnie.*

DIRECTIONS: Insert commas where needed in each sentence below. If commas are not needed, write "OK" in front of the sentence.

Example: *The county, so I hear, is raising the sales tax again.*

1. Our oldest male relative who will be ninety-five this April lives in Manitoba.

2. Crossing the Atlantic in a small sailboat is quite a feat even if your name is Christopher Columbus.

3. Lee said gloomily "We cannot afford a vacation this year."

4. Any salesperson who exceeds his or her quota will receive a bonus.

5. You can expect your check to arrive by Tuesday but not sooner.

6. Jane leaving the home in which she grew up turned to her family and said "This is the start of a new life for me."

7. "The more money I make" said Joe "the more money I owe."

8. We will of course repair the damaged television set free of charge.

Answers begin on page 65.

Exercise 30   COMMA REVIEW

DIRECTIONS: Check each of the following sentences for errors in the
use of commas. If there is a mistake, blacken the space
over the number corresponding to it in the answer grid.
If there is no error, blacken the space numbered (5).

Example: Since the recession, the unemployment rate, has risen
to its highest level in forty years.

○ ● ○ ○ ○
1 2 3 4 5

1. One of the strangest sights I'd ever seen was Uncle Jake
wearing a hat, that belonged to his sister.

1. ○ ○ ○ ○ ○
1 2 3 4 5

2. Bring your bathing suit, and a towel, but don't bother
with a change of clothes. In fact, we may not even go to
the beach.

2. ○ ○ ○ ○ ○
1 2 3 4 5

3. Susan, who is studying to become a doctor, will help us
paint the apartment if we tell her that we need her help.

3. ○ ○ ○ ○ ○
1 2 3 4 5

4. Although the couple lived together for five years, from
September 10, 1980, to January 25, 1986 they never
actually married.

4. ○ ○ ○ ○ ○
1 2 3 4 5

5. If I run out, before telling the truth, will I ever be able to
face him again? On the other hand, why would I want to
see him again?

5. ○ ○ ○ ○ ○
1 2 3 4 5

6. This is, I am sure you realize, an illegal immoral, and
unhealthy activity.

6. ○ ○ ○ ○ ○
1 2 3 4 5

7. Relax, Jonas, you have $1,000 in the bank not $100.

7. ○ ○ ○ ○ ○
1 2 3 4 5

8. Tell me Delores, if you see a mysterious man wearing
a blue shirt.

8. ○ ○ ○ ○ ○
1 2 3 4 5

9. Spring is nice and cool but many people like fall's
crispness even better.

9. ○ ○ ○ ○ ○
1 2 3 4 5

Answers begin on page 65.

Exercise 31 THE SEMICOLON I

Follow the rules in this and the next exercise to use the semicolon correctly:

1) Use a semicolon between two sentences joined by a conjunctive adverb, such as *consequently, moreover, furthermore, indeed, still, then, however, therefore, nevertheless, thus,* etc.

>   You have good ideas; *however,* you must express them more clearly.

(Note that a comma goes after a conjunctive adverb joining sentences.)

DIRECTIONS: Combine each pair of sentences below into one compound sentence using an appropriate conjunctive adverb and the proper punctuation. For some sentences, there may be more than one correct answer.

Example: The main bank opens at 8:00. The loan department doesn't open until 9:00.

The main bank opens at 8:00; however, the loan department doesn't open until 9:00.

1. Marty's sister died of lung cancer. He always urges his friends to quit smoking.

   _____

2. Your illness is very contagious. Wash the thermometer well.

   _____

3. The wedding itself will be small. There will be a huge reception when the couple return from their honeymoon.

   _____

4. Mix all the ingredients. Pour the batter in a cake pan.

   _____

5. Mattie has cataracts in both eyes. She is completely deaf in one ear.

   _____

6. Jack and I broke up last week. I have to admit that I love him.

   _____

7. In general, small cars get good gas mileage. Many have front-wheel drive to assure good handling on ice and snow.

   _____

8. Courtney plans to be a lawyer. She plans to have a family.

   _____

Answers begin on page 65.

Exercise 32 THE SEMICOLON II

Also use the semicolon in these ways:

2) To combine two closely related complete sentences that are not joined together by a conjunction.

> *The governor was reelected by a landslide; his opponent didn't have a chance.*

3) To separate items in a list when commas alone would be confusing.

> I made a list of favorite foods and their origins: *pasta, Italian; curry, Indian; enchiladas, Mexican;* and *chocolate soufflé, French.*

DIRECTIONS: Insert semicolons and commas where needed in the following sentences.

Example: The suit is out of style; I need a new one.

1. The snow is falling steadily it appears we're in for a blizzard.

2. Mrs. Davis is proud of her sons and daughters: Howard the computer programmer Janice the engineer Glenn the teacher and Belinda the beautician.

3. The meeting is important please be there.

4. The Pistons scored six baskets in a row they seemed to have the court to themselves.

5. Mac will bring potato chips onion dip and guacamole Judy will bring an assortment of cheeses and Ted will bring soft drinks.

6. Damp weather is bad for people with arthritis many such people move to Arizona because of its dry climate.

7. The sky was gloomy on the day of the funeral it rained and rained.

8. The salesman's territory covers Rochester Minnesota Chicago Illinois and Milwaukee Wisconsin.

9. Please call us we need to speak with you.

10. There are many good coupons in today's paper I plan to use every one!

Answers begin on page 65.

Exercise 33   SEMICOLON AND COMMA REVIEW

> **DIRECTIONS:** Check each of the following sentences for errors in the use of semicolons and commas. If there is a mistake, blacken the space over the number corresponding to it in the answer grid. If there is no error, blacken the space numbered (5).

Example: Joseph, our distant cousin, traces his roots back to
    ¹   ²
Vienna, Austria, both of his grandparents were born
    ³   ⁴
there.

⃝ ⃝ ⃝ ● ⃝
1 2 3 4 5

1. Please meet my husband, Richard; my son, Evan; and my
                          ¹   ²   ³
    daughter; Sylvia.
            ⁴

1. ⃝ ⃝ ⃝ ⃝ ⃝
   1 2 3 4 5

2. Sandy, you are a dreamer; consequently, you come up
       ¹   ²   ³
    with some very, creative ideas.
                  ⁴

2. ⃝ ⃝ ⃝ ⃝ ⃝
   1 2 3 4 5

3. The flight attendant warned, "Fasten your seat belts." She
                               ¹
    continued, "The air is turbulent; and we may be tossed
              ²   ³   ⁴
    around a bit."

3. ⃝ ⃝ ⃝ ⃝ ⃝
   1 2 3 4 5

4. This has been a miserable, disastrous, and totally
                             ¹   ²
    unbearable day, indeed, it has been a horrible week.
                  ³   ⁴

4. ⃝ ⃝ ⃝ ⃝ ⃝
   1 2 3 4 5

5. Because he goes to bed early, eats moderately, and
                                ¹   ²
    exercises regularly, Ahmad is healthy, and fit.
                       ³   ⁴

5. ⃝ ⃝ ⃝ ⃝ ⃝
   1 2 3 4 5

6. The Chicago Symphony Orchestra, which is one of the
                                  ¹
    best in the country, rehearses four times a week, not
                       ²   ³
    three; this contributes to its excellence.
         ⁴

6. ⃝ ⃝ ⃝ ⃝ ⃝
   1 2 3 4 5

7. If the weather is good, the picnic will be May 28th;
                         ¹   ²   ³
    however; we are not too hopeful.
           ⁴

7. ⃝ ⃝ ⃝ ⃝ ⃝
   1 2 3 4 5

8. Having trouble sleeping, is a nightmare in itself; it makes
                          ¹   ²
    you nervous, groggy, and often irritable.
              ³   ⁴

8. ⃝ ⃝ ⃝ ⃝ ⃝
   1 2 3 4 5

9. Today as you know, is primary election day, and voter
        ¹   ²   ³
    turnout is predicted to be quite high.
                                    ⁴

9. ⃝ ⃝ ⃝ ⃝ ⃝
   1 2 3 4 5

Answers begin on page 65.

Exercise 34   THE COLON

Use the colon in these ways:

1) Before a list of items, if the words preceding the list form a complete sentence.

   The supplies are ready: blankets, a thermos, mosquito nets, sleeping bags, and a portable radio.

2) Between hours and minutes in clock time.

   7:45   5:32

3) After the salutation of a business letter.

   Dear Governor Thompson: Dear Sir or Madam:

4) Before rules or guidelines introduced by words such as *note, remember,* or *important.*

   Note: Everyone must attend the meeting.

DIRECTIONS: In each of the following sentences, insert colons, semicolons, and/or commas where needed.

Example: I do the following chores:cook three meals, wash dishes, and take out the garbage.

1. Learn to spell the words in List I *receive believe thief neighbor* and *weigh.*

2. Dear Representative Luhm

3. You must return at 300 therefore you have two hours to shop.

4. Important Keep the doors locked after business hours.

5. People of all ages are welcome toddlers children teens adults and senior citizens.

6. Dear Sir or Madam
   In the enclosed package are five unordered items one umbrella two rainhats one pair of gloves and one folding raincoat.

7. The items you need are as follows paper pencils and an eraser.

8. The members voted for the following officers secretary treasurer vice-president and sergeant-at-arms.

9. Don't show up before 900 because the doors will be locked.

10. Remember The election will be held this Tuesday.

Answers begin on page 65.

Exercise 35   THE APOSTROPHE I

Use the apostrophe to show ownership in these ways:

1) Add *'s* to a singular person or thing, even if the word ends in *s*.

> *Jess's* dogs

> the *car's* brake system

2) Add the apostrophe alone (') to a plural that ends in *s*.

> the *Smiths'* daughters

> my *in-laws'* house

3) Add *'s* to a plural not ending in *s*.

> *women's* rights

> the *people's* choice

> **Note:** Pronouns show possession without an apostrophe.

> *hers, his, its, theirs, ours, yours, whose*

DIRECTIONS: Use the words below to write phrases. Write the correct possessive form of the first noun.

Example: Tyrell/diploma *Tyrell's diploma*

1. Mrs. Kelly/job _____
2. the men/room _____
3. Dr. Kraus/office _____
4. the unions/pension plans _____
5. her company/benefits _____
6. the teachers/meeting room _____
7. ladies/shoes _____
8. my boss/personality _____
9. Ms. Sosa/car _____
10. the Sosas/landlord _____
11. the children/drawings _____
12. babies/outfits _____

EXTRA PRACTICE

Write five sentences about people you know. Include a possessive noun in each sentence. (So that your instructor can check the possessive forms, indicate in parentheses how many people you are talking about.)

Examples: *My* aunts' *sons are both bilingual. (2 aunts)*

> The supervisor's *job is tough. (1 supervisor)*

Answers begin on page 66.

Exercise 36   THE APOSTROPHE II

Also use an apostrophe in these situations:

4) To show that a letter has been left out of a contraction.

   wasn't (was not), *what's* (what is), *I'm* (I am)

5) To show the plural of numbers or uncapitalized letters.

   Joe often forgets to dot his *i's*.

   Mary's *2's* and *3's* look almost alike.

   Note: In all other situations, it is incorrect to use an apostrophe with a nonpossessive plural noun:

   WRONG: My *cousins'* ate all the *hot dog's* and *french fry's*.

   RIGHT: My *cousins* ate all the *hot dogs* and *french fries*.

DIRECTIONS: Using rules 1–5, insert apostrophes where needed to show possession, contractions, or plurals of numbers and letters.

Example: Don't send Casey's mail to her parents' home—it's private.

1. A persons worth shouldnt be measured by his or her bank balance.

2. Jackies handwriting is terrible; her *u*s, *v*s, and *w*s all look the same.

3. Cant anyone drive Mrs. Kubik to her doctors office? She needs to see him, and Im certain shes too weak to go alone.

4. Ill call Lynettes office as soon as the phone lines are clear.

5. Our sons teachers are working with him on his speech sounds, especially his *ing*s and *th*s.

6. Whats the name of the new student? Its important that I know.

7. Pretzels, potato chips, cookies, and greasy hamburgers are my childrens favorite foods; I cant get them to eat any vegetables.

8. We didnt know whether to believe what the three boys had told us; the boys version of yesterdays events was quite different from the mens version.

EXTRA PRACTICE

Write sentences using each of the following contractions:

doesn't, don't, didn't, isn't, wasn't, weren't, can't, won't.

Answers begin on page 66.

Exercise 37 PUNCTUATION REVIEW

> **DIRECTIONS:** Check each of the following sentences for errors in the use of periods, question marks, exclamation marks, commas, semicolons, colons, and apostrophes. If there is a mistake, blacken the space over the number corresponding to it in the answer grid. If there is no error, blacken the space numbered (5).

Example: The meeting, that you missed began at 4:00; you'll
have to find out what was discussed.

●○○○○
1 2 3 4 5

1. "Be quiet, gentlemen and ladies !" barked the teacher. "This is a math class not a shouting contest."

1. ○○○○○
   1 2 3 4 5

2. If you cant come today, tomorrow is okay, too.

2. ○○○○○
   1 2 3 4 5

3. The gift set contained everything: after-shave lotion; shaving cream, deodorant, and talcum powder.

3. ○○○○○
   1 2 3 4 5

4. Barbara and Melvin are going to adopt a baby, therefore, they will soon have a son or daughter to love and raise.

4. ○○○○○
   1 2 3 4 5

5. Please, Greg, try to be quiet; you know that your noise ruins everyones concentration.

5. ○○○○○
   1 2 3 4 5

6. Whenever a book becomes a bestseller television or movie producers think about turning it into a TV show or a film.

6. ○○○○○
   1 2 3 4 5

7. Rosa, can't come over tonight; nevertheless, she will call.

7. ○○○○○
   1 2 3 4 5

8. Whats the matter with Kyle? Doesn't he feel well?

8. ○○○○○
   1 2 3 4 5

9. As soon as the plane took off, the pilot's voice came over the loudspeaker to explain the delay; he told us we were being hijacked.

9. ○○○○○
   1 2 3 4 5

(continued)

10. Are you sure about the menu? I think the Merrills are
 vegetarians ; and I know Bo dislikes pork.

10. ◯ ◯ ◯ ◯ ◯
  1 2 3 4 5

11. The cupboards shelves are well stocked: food, cleaning
 supplies, and plenty of paper goods are all there.

11. ◯ ◯ ◯ ◯ ◯
  1 2 3 4 5

12. In the fall, temperatures may drop in a hurry,
 nonetheless, it's my favorite time of the year.

12. ◯ ◯ ◯ ◯ ◯
  1 2 3 4 5

13. The clocks say 8:22; we must've lost power during last
 nights storm.

13. ◯ ◯ ◯ ◯ ◯
  1 2 3 4 5

14. The fall colors were splendid: brown, red, gold, and
 burgundy.

14. ◯ ◯ ◯ ◯ ◯
  1 2 3 4 5

15. Claire, no one in our family, has a history of diabetes, at
 least not that I know of.

15. ◯ ◯ ◯ ◯ ◯
  1 2 3 4 5

16. I wonder why Linda doesn't talk to Joshua's teacher?

16. ◯ ◯ ◯ ◯ ◯
  1 2 3 4 5

17. Youre a rat! I trusted you, but you've let me down one
 time too many.

17. ◯ ◯ ◯ ◯ ◯
  1 2 3 4 5

18. Which of the Silvers' cat's do you like best?

18. ◯ ◯ ◯ ◯ ◯
  1 2 3 4 5

19. The animal trainer, while holding a whip in her right
 hand, instructed the beasts to: lie down and roll over.

19. ◯ ◯ ◯ ◯ ◯
  1 2 3 4 5

20. Seventy-five peoples names on the petition won't get the
 item on the ballot; you'll have to get more signatures.

20. ◯ ◯ ◯ ◯ ◯
  1 2 3 4 5

Answers begin on page 66.

Exercise 38   QUOTATION MARKS I

Place quotation marks around a speaker's exact words:

> *"Let's go to the movies,"* said Miss Farrell.

Placement of Commas
When a quotation that is not a question or an exclamation comes before the rest of the sentence, a comma is placed at the end of the quotation, inside the quotation marks. However, when the quotation ends the sentence, the comma is placed before the quotation to separate the speaker from his or her words:

> *"Come on,"* said Julie.

> Her brother responded, *"Right away, Sis."*

Placement of End Punctuation
Periods always go inside quotation marks and can only be used when the quotation ends the sentence.

> I said, *"Try to call again."*

If the quoted words are a question or an exclamation, the end punctuation goes inside the quotation marks. However, when the quotation is a statement, but the sentence as a whole is a question or exclamation, then the end punctuation goes outside the quotation marks.

> *"What's the problem?"* asked Paul.

> Who said, *"I have the answer"*?

Notice that in the first quotation directly above, a comma does not separate the speaker from his words. A comma is not used if a quotation at the beginning of a sentence requires a question or exclamation mark.

DIRECTIONS: In the following sentences, insert quotation marks and other punctuation where needed.

Example: *"Do you think it's hot in here?"* asked Mariel.

1. Harry said This is the nut and bolt assembly for the latch

2. How do you know asked his assistant

3. Because it's labeled clearly explained Harry

4. The less-experienced worker asked How could I have missed that

5. Who said We're all in big trouble

6. Weren't the Marx Brothers' old routines funny asked Belle

7. Are you ready to order asked the waiter

8. The mail carrier said There is twelve cents postage due on this letter

9. The theater manager shouted No smoking is allowed

10. Isn't that an informative article asked the librarian

Answers begin on page 66.

Exercise 39   QUOTATION MARKS II

When punctuating quotations, distinguish between direct quotations and indirect quotations. A **direct quotation** states the exact words as spoken, while an **indirect quotation** summarizes the idea of the quotation. Only direct quotations require quotation marks.

Direct: Olga asked, *"Do you need a ride?"*

Indirect: Olga asked *if I needed a ride.*

Sometimes a quotation is divided. A **divided quotation** is one in which the words that name the speaker interrupt or separate the exact words being quoted. Study the examples below for correct punctuation of divided quotations.

"Why in the world," wondered Delia, *"would anyone watch so much TV?"*

"Think about the problem," encouraged the teacher. *"Then try to come up with a solution of your own."*

DIRECTIONS: Read each sentence below and decide if it is correct as written or if it requires quotation marks. If the sentence is correct, write "OK" on the blank. If the sentence requires quotation marks, write them in where they are needed. Insert other punctuation or capitalization necessary for correct quotations.

Example: *"Look the word up in the dictionary,"* said his boss.   _____

1. Someone called and asked if this was the Chinese restaurant.   1. _____

2. I told them to look in the telephone book for the correct number.   2. _____

3. On holiday weekends drive very carefully cautioned Paula.   3. _____

4. For all you know said Cecile that could have been a burglar trying to see if anyone was at home.   4. _____

5. Let's drop the subject pleaded Amanda I don't even want to think about it.   5. _____

6. Do you want another cup of coffee offered David or would a glass of milk calm your nerves?   6. _____

7. *Time* magazine's movie reviewer said that the film was marvelous.   7. _____

8. By all means, let's see it suggested Leopold.   8. _____

9. People always ask my sister if she dyes her hair or if her hair is naturally red.   9. _____

10. Let's ask the folks if they'd like to come to dinner this Sunday.   10. _____

Answers begin on page 66.

Exercise 40   QUOTATION MARKS III

Use quotation marks around titles of shorter written pieces: essays, short stories, articles, chapters, poems, and songs:

I love Edgar Allan Poe's poem, *"The Raven."*

My all-time favorite Springsteen song is *"Thunder Road."*

Note: Never use quotation marks simply to emphasize a word or words. Instead, use underlining or italics for emphasis.

WRONG: We "really care" about our students.

RIGHT: We *really care* about our students.

> **DIRECTIONS:** In the following sentences, insert quotation marks and any other necessary punctuation. Also change lower-case (small) letters to capital letters if necessary.

Example: Whenever I hear the song "Stop in the Name of Love" on the oldies station, I have to get up and dance.

1. Do you remember when Mom sang The Star-Spangled Banner at my Little League game I was absolutely mortified!

2. Lia asked the teacher do you think I am really ready to take the GED test

3. How should I know responded her brother you never tell me what's going on

4. Did you read the article It's a Matter of Time in last week's *Journal* It was fascinating

5. Who shouted fire in the crowded theater

6. Lying on the beach while listening to the radio is one of my favorite summertime activities Carlos told Gina

7. Do you know the words to the song Rhythm Nation by Janet Jackson.

8. Even though the assignment required that all of us use the same title, Trying to Change the Things We Can't, all the essays turned out quite differently

---

EXTRA PRACTICE

Copy and complete each sentence using correct punctuation:

1. My favorite song is . . .

2. If someone wrote a short story about my life, it would be called . . .

Answers begin on page 67.

Exercise 41 QUOTATION MARKS REVIEW

Example: Mrs. Venard said, "Come on, children. It's time to clean up." ⊙

1. "What time is it?" asked the driver?

2. Laurie asked "why we had left so early.

3. The director said, "Take five!"

4. The sign in the window said, "Sale on "genuine" leather coats."

5. "Hi, fellows," Said Mr. Maxwell. "What's going on?"

6. Eli, you shouldn't have taken me to your parents' home.

7. I "can't stand" it when my sister cracks her knuckles; she really knows how to get to me!

8. Who told Megan "that she should sing "Home on the Range" at the top of her lungs?

9. "When the refrigerator door opens." explained the repairman, "the motor works harder."

10. "If you ask me," said Vanessa, "he wants a maid instead of a wife."

11. "Today," the coach warned his players, "Will be our last full practice before the big game."

12. "Don't the pines smell terrific," asked Daisy.

13. I'm not sure who wrote "The Moonlight Sonata".

Answers begin on page 67.

Exercise 42   PUNCTUATION REVIEW

> **DIRECTIONS:** In each of the following sentences, four marks of punctuation or spaces between words have been underlined. If one of these marks of punctuation is incorrect, or if some necessary punctuation is missing, blacken the space over the number corresponding to it in the answer grid. If all the punctuation is correct, blacken the space numbered (5).

Example: *It's hard to work on one's chore's on Fridays.*
 <u>1</u>   <u>2</u>   <u>3</u>   <u>4</u>

○ ○ ● ○ ○
1 2 3 4 5

1. We've called the store's manager, however, she has not
    replied.

    1. ○ ○ ○ ○ ○
       1 2 3 4 5

2. "Are you joking? " asked Danillo?

    2. ○ ○ ○ ○ ○
       1 2 3 4 5

3. The wind, I see, has died down: let's make a run for it!

    3. ○ ○ ○ ○ ○
       1 2 3 4 5

4. Though they'd been deserted on the island for six
    months, the crew members looked rested, well-fed, and
    happy, to be rescued.

    4. ○ ○ ○ ○ ○
       1 2 3 4 5

5. Bert who has just moved in upstairs, always wears
    metal-toed shoes; they really make a racket.

    5. ○ ○ ○ ○ ○
       1 2 3 4 5

6. "This rash is killing me! " exclaimed Nina!

    6. ○ ○ ○ ○ ○
       1 2 3 4 5

7. The childrens' room needs painting, but we just don't
    have the money, I'm afraid.

    7. ○ ○ ○ ○ ○
       1 2 3 4 5

8. "The employee's first months at a company," stated Ms.
    Jones the personnel manager, "are considered a learning
    period."

    8. ○ ○ ○ ○ ○
       1 2 3 4 5

9. People, who eat a lot of eggs must watch their
    cholesterol levels; they may run the risk of premature
    heart attacks.

    9. ○ ○ ○ ○ ○
       1 2 3 4 5

10. Tracy Chapmans first album contains two great songs:
    "Fast Car" and "Across the Lines."

    10. ○ ○ ○ ○ ○
        1 2 3 4 5

(continued)

11. The sergeant said ‾ "that he wanted to see the men's
    ‾1 ‾2   ‾3
    boots.
    ‾4

11. ○ ○ ○ ○ ○
    1 2 3 4 5

12. Cassandra, our youngest child, is learning to write, but
              ‾1   ‾2   ‾3
    she sometimes writes her b's backwards.
                          ‾4

12. ○ ○ ○ ○ ○
    1 2 3 4 5

13. Sir, you have your shoes on the wrong feet, I'm almost
    ‾1   ‾2 ‾3
    too embarrassed to mention this.
                              ‾4

13. ○ ○ ○ ○ ○
    1 2 3 4 5

14. No‾no one here, at least to my knowledge, called the
    ‾1   ‾2   ‾3
    police‾or fire department.
    ‾4

14. ○ ○ ○ ○ ○
    1 2 3 4 5

15. The family's grocery order was tremendous: twenty-five
              ‾1   ‾2
    pounds of meat, six dozen eggs, and, four gallons of milk.
              ‾3   ‾4

15. ○ ○ ○ ○ ○
    1 2 3 4 5

16. Which one of your neighbors has the biggest family?
                          ‾1   ‾2
    Lonnie, Sam, or Nate?
          ‾3   ‾4

16. ○ ○ ○ ○ ○
    1 2 3 4 5

17. Did you know‾that Richard Petty‾won the Daytona 500‾
               ‾1   ‾2   ‾3
    at least seven times in a twenty-year period?
                                           ‾4

17. ○ ○ ○ ○ ○
    1 2 3 4 5

18. When I take my vacation, I'll visit my sister in
    Charlottesville, my cousin in Tampa, and my brother at
                  ‾1   ‾2
    Ft. Harrison‾Indiana.
    ‾3   ‾4

18. ○ ○ ○ ○ ○
    1 2 3 4 5

19. Child abuse is a terrible problem‾it has been shown‾that
                                    ‾1   ‾2
    when unemployment increases, child abuse also
                              ‾3
    increases.
    ‾4

19. ○ ○ ○ ○ ○
    1 2 3 4 5

20. Its a major crisis, Cagney. How will we ever be able to
    ‾1   ‾2   ‾3
    keep the groups at peace‾if they won't agree to this
                            ‾4
    meeting?

20. ○ ○ ○ ○ ○
    1 2 3 4 5

Answers begin on page 67.

FINAL SKILLS INVENTORY

Part I   SPELLING

> **DIRECTIONS:** In each set of words, find the misspelled word. No set has more than one error. Blacken the space in the answer grid over the number that corresponds to the misspelled word. If there is no error, blacken the space numbered (5).

Example: (1) impractical (2) driving (3) illegible (4) writeing

1.   (1) neither   (2) decieve   (3) chief   (4) believe
2.   (1) earlyer   (2) decoys   (3) decaying   (4) sorrier
3.   (1) enemy   (2) medecal   (3) mineral   (4) tragedy
4.   (1) immature   (2) unequal   (3) iresponsible   (4) unnatural
5.   (1) liability   (2) dialy   (3) diameter   (4) faint
6.   (1) fallen   (2) trailler   (3) teller   (4) failing
7.   (1) advantage   (2) divorce   (3) avrage   (4) devilish
8.   (1) promotion   (2) procedure   (3) procclaim   (4) progress
9.   (1) announcment   (2) apartment   (3) argument   (4) pavement
10. (1) actual   (2) situation   (3) consideration   (4) intelectual
11. (1) sizzle   (2) fuzzy   (3) dozzen   (4) pizza
12. (1) yearly   (2) cereal   (3) already   (4) beaneth
13. (1) mischief   (2) thief   (3) either   (4) neighbor
14. (1) stares   (2) stairs   (3) wait   (4) waight
15. (1) salaried   (2) studying   (3) prettier   (4) holidaies
16. (1) scenery   (2) desend   (3) nonsense   (4) school
17. (1) bookkends   (2) bookkeeping   (3) roommate   (4) shirttail
18. (1) buttered   (2) ordered   (3) wanderred   (4) inferred
19. (1) clatter   (2) congrattulate   (3) collateral   (4) Saturday
20. (1) unpleasesant   (2) unsweetened   (3) immaterial   (4) immature

(continued)

Part II CAPITALIZATION AND PUNCTUATION

> **DIRECTIONS:** Some of the following sentences contain errors in capitalization and punctuation. If there is an error, select the one underlined part that must be changed to make the sentence correct. Blacken the numbered space in the answer grid that corresponds to the error. If there is no error, blacken the space numbered (5). No sentence contains more than one error.

Example: John Goodman, who plays the role of Roseanne's Husband, Dan, is
1   2 3   4

a natural comedian.

     ○ ○ ● ○ ○
     1 2 3 4 5

21. Until the new clubhouse is completed, we will meet at Bertha's
                         1   2

Diner which is located in downtown Harvey.
  3   4

21. ○ ○ ○ ○ ○
    1 2 3 4 5

22. Each morning the sun rises in the East, and each evening it sets in
                              1 2

the west; we can be certain of that.
   3 4

22. ○ ○ ○ ○ ○
    1 2 3 4 5

23. "You must, " ordered the judge "respond to the question."
       1 2   3 4

23. ○ ○ ○ ○ ○
    1 2 3 4 5

24. Do you know when Dr. Martin Luther King, Jr., was born.
        1   2   3   4

24. ○ ○ ○ ○ ○
    1 2 3 4 5

25. My old Sears typewriter has the following problems; the keys stick,
       1   2   3

the ribbon slips, and the margins do not hold.
        4

25. ○ ○ ○ ○ ○
    1 2 3 4 5

26. When the troops paraded down Pennsylvania Avenue, the general
                    1   2   3   4

reviewed their formations.

26. ○ ○ ○ ○ ○
    1 2 3 4 5

27. Some of Liptons many varieties of soup are in the cafeteria's vending
      1   2   3   4

machine.

27. ○ ○ ○ ○ ○
    1 2 3 4 5

28. When dad turns sixty-five, his wife will be only sixty, or so she says.
      1   2   3   4

28. ○ ○ ○ ○ ○
    1 2 3 4 5

29. Deborah said " that she'd be happy to be a bridesmaid at Tanya's
            1 2   3

wedding.
    4

29. ○ ○ ○ ○ ○
    1 2 3 4 5

(continued)

30. Grace's fiancé speaks little english; nevertheless, they communicate
    <u> </u>
    1   2   3   4

    beautifully.

30. ○ ○ ○ ○ ○
    1 2 3 4 5

31. "All hands on deck! This is an emergency! " shouted captain Vere.
                    1   2   3   4

31. ○ ○ ○ ○ ○
    1 2 3 4 5

32. The librarian told us the references were lost or stolen, therefore, we
        1   2   3

    are requesting an extension on the assignment, Professor.
                                                   4

32. ○ ○ ○ ○ ○
    1 2 3 4 5

33. On St. Patrick's day, my neighbors gather at the local pub, have a
                     1   2

    beer, and sing "When Irish Eyes Are Smiling."
        3   4

33. ○ ○ ○ ○ ○
    1 2 3 4 5

34. Please don't bring home *Raiders of the lost Ark* from the video store
                            1   2   3

    again; we've seen it four times.
    4

34. ○ ○ ○ ○ ○
    1 2 3 4 5

35. She probably didn't realize that you were meeting her at 6:45
                    1   2 3

    Susan," said Marsha's husband.
                          4

35. ○ ○ ○ ○ ○
    1 2 3 4 5

36. If you'll drive me to the bus depot tomorrow morning I'll even let
        1   2   3

    you pick me up early on Friday evening.
                           4

36. ○ ○ ○ ○ ○
    1 2 3 4 5

37. Amber, Im going to need the following items for tomorrow's dinner:
          1 2   3

    spaghetti, hamburger meat, Coke, and ice cream.
                               4

37. ○ ○ ○ ○ ○
    1 2 3 4 5

38. It's too early to tell who the winner will be, Jason Cohen, Carrie Ann
      1   2   3   4

    Jones, or Stacy Robinson.

38. ○ ○ ○ ○ ○
    1 2 3 4 5

39. The only witness's testimony was heard at 10:00; at noon, the jury
                 1   2   3

    read the verdict in front of the Judge.
                                     4

39. ○ ○ ○ ○ ○
    1 2 3 4 5

40. The best chili in the world is found at Francesca's Chili pot Inn at
                                                        1   2   3

    the southeast corner of Junction and Ames Streets.
        4

40. ○ ○ ○ ○ ○
    1 2 3 4 5

Answers and Explanations begin on page 57.

FINAL SKILLS INVENTORY EVALUATION CHART

> **DIRECTIONS:** After completing the Final Skills Inventory, check your answers by using the Final Skills Inventory Answers and Explanations, pages 57–58. Write the total number of *correct* answers for each skill area on the blank lines below. If you have *more than one incorrect* answer in any skill area, review the appropriate exercises. The chart shows you which workbook exercises you'll need to review.

Skill Area	Item Numbers	Total	Number Correct	Exercise Numbers
Part I Spelling	1–20	20	_____	1–14
Part II Capitalization	22, 28, 30, 31, 33, 34, 39, 40	8	_____	15–24
End punctuation	24	1	_____	25–26
Commas	21, 23, 35, 36	4	_____	27–30, 33
Semicolons	32	1	_____	31–33, 37
Colons	25, 38	2	_____	34, 37
Apostrophes	27, 37	2	_____	35–37
Quotation marks	29	1	_____	38–42

Note: Items 13 and 26 are correct.

Answers and Explanations   FINAL SKILLS INVENTORY

> **DIRECTIONS:** After completing the Final Skills Inventory (pages 53–55), use these Answers and Explanations to check your work. *On these pages,* circle the number of each item you correctly answered. Then turn to the Final Skills Inventory Evaluation Chart (page 56) and follow the directions given.

Part I   SPELLING

1. **(2)** deceive — The *"i* before *e* except after *c"* rule applies here.

2. **(1)** earlier — In words ending in *y* after a consonant, the *y* is changed to *i* before a suffix (unless the suffix begins with *i*).

3. **(2)** medical — The unstressed second vowel in *medical* is spelled with *i*, not *e.*

4. **(3)** irresponsible — This word is made up of the prefix *ir* plus the base word *responsible.* Therefore, the letter *r* appears twice.

5. **(2)** daily — The correct vowel pattern for this word is *ai.* It has the same sound as the *ai* combination in *faint.*

6. **(2)** trailer — When adding a vowel suffix, double the final consonant of a one-syllable word only when the word ends in one vowel and one consonant. The base word *trail* has two vowels: *a* and *i.*

7. **(3)** average — Pronouncing this word in syllables will help you to remember that it has three syllables: *av /er /age .*

8. **(3)** proclaim — This word is made up of the prefix *pro* plus the base word *claim.* Therefore, there is no double consonant.

9. **(1)** announcement — Generally, the silent *e* at the end of a word (*announce*) is kept when a consonant suffix is added.

10. **(4)** intellectual — Pronouncing this word in syllables will help you to remember that it contains two *l*'s: *in/tel/lec/tu/al.*

11. **(3)** dozen — This word contains only one *z.*

12. **(4)** beneath — This word contains only one *ea* combination, and it follows the *n.*

13. **(5)** No error

14. **(4)** weight — *Weight*, the homonym for *wait*, contains the vowel combination *ei*, not *ai*

15. **(4)** holidays — In words ending in *y* after a vowel, the *y* is always kept when a suffix is added.

16. **(2)** descend — The *c* is silent, as in *scenery.*

17. **(1)** bookends — This compound word is made up of the words *book* and *ends;* therefore, there is no double letter.

(continued)

18. **(3)** wandered — The stress is not on the last syllable of the base word *wander;* therefore, do not double the final consonant before adding a suffix.

19. **(2)** congratulate — Pronouncing the word in syllables will help you to remember that it does not have a double *t: con / grat /u /late.*

20. **(1)** unpleasant — If you read the word exactly as it was incorrectly spelled, you will hear that an extra syllable was added: "un /pleas /ES /ant." The correctly spelled word has only three syllables: *un /pleas /ant.*

Part II   CAPITALIZATION AND PUNCTUATION

21. **(3)** A comma is needed here because the clause *which is located in downtown Harvey* does not add essential information to the sentence. Regardless of where it is located, we know we are talking about the one and only Bertha's Diner.

22. **(1)** When *east* is used as a direction, it should not be capitalized.

23. **(3)** A comma is needed here to set off the speaker from her exact words.

24. **(4)** Use a question mark, not a period, at the end of a question.

25. **(2)** A colon, not a semicolon, is used before a list of items.

26. **(5)** No error

27. **(2)** *Lipton's* should have an apostrophe in order to show possession.

28. **(1)** *Dad* should be capitalized since it is taking the place of a person's name.

29. **(1)** Quotation marks should not be used because the quotation is indirect.

30. **(2)** Names of languages should be capitalized: *English.*

31. **(4)** Capitalize special titles when they are being used as part of a name: *Captain Vere.*

32. **(2)** A semicolon, not a comma, is used to combine two closely related sentences joined by a conjunctive adverb such as *therefore.*

33. **(1)** Capitalize entire names of holidays: *St. Patrick's Day.*

34. **(1)** Capitalize all important words in titles: *Raiders of the Lost Ark.*

35. **(3)** Use a comma to set off the name of the person being addressed.

36. **(3)** A comma is needed after an introductory clause when the rest of the sentence could stand alone as a separate sentence.

37. **(2)** An apostrophe is needed here to form the contraction of *I am: I'm.*

38. **(3)** Use a colon before a list of items if the words preceding the list could stand alone as a sentence.

39. **(4)** Do not capitalize *judge* in this sentence. Only capitalize a job title if it is being used in place of a name or as part of a name.

40. **(2)** Capitalize specific names of places: Francesca's Chili Pot Inn.

ANSWER KEY

EXERCISE 1

1. com/mu/ni/ty
2. en/vi/ron/ment
3. li/quor
4. ath/lete
5. in/sti/tu/tion
6. tem/per/a/ture
7. to/mor/row
8. com/mit/ted
9. dif/fer/ent
10. priv/i/lege
11. gov/ern/ment
12. jew/el/ry

EXERCISE 2

1. convenient
2. presentation
3. combination
4. OK
5. exactly
6. unusual
7. responsible
8. irrelevant
9. advantages
10. explain
11. lawyer
12. library
13. furniture
14. OK
15. economical

EXERCISE 3

1. 3
2. 3
3. 2
4. 1
5. 5
6. 2
7. 1
8. 3
9. 2
10. 1
11. 5
12. 1
13. 2
14. 3
15. 2

EXERCISE 4

1. neighbor's
2. relief
3. perceive
4. mischief
5. receiver
6. piece
7. OK
8. sieges

EXERCISE 5

1. 2
2. 5
3. 3
4. 1
5. 5
6. 3
7. 2
8. 5
9. 2
10. 2
11. 4
12. 2
13. 1
14. 3

EXERCISE 6

1. weekend
2. roommate
3. heavyweight
4. barroom
5. shareholder
6. reincarnation
7. mismanage
8. preregister
9. prorated
10. inconvenient
11. unfold
12. illegible
13. supersonic
14. semimonthly
15. irregular
1. OK
2. bookkeeper
3. OK
4. OK
5. headstrong
6. OK
7. dissatisfied
8. immaterial
9. reemploy
10. OK
11. OK
12. inedible
13. OK
14. OK
15. irrelevant

EXERCISE 7

1. annoys
2. finely
3. blameless
4. attaches
5. flies
6. craziness
7. payment
8. plentiful
9. resists
10. painfully
1. OK
2. babies
3. commitment
4. truly
5. OK
6. fries
7. argument
8. OK
9. worries
10. watches

EXERCISE 8

1. listener
2. tried
3. desirable
4. trapped
5. revealed
6. sleepier
7. annoyance
8. biodegradable
9. sloppiest
10. expelled
11. advantageous
12. limited

EXERCISE 9

1. seems, hurrying
2. wondered, sadness
3. ladies, daintily, sipped
4. OK, enabling
5. OK, walking, OK
6. plays, toys, excited, racing, cars
7. truly, likely, commitment
8. sincerely, OK, OK, remarks, OK

60

EXERCISE 10

1.	3	11.	3
2.	5	12.	4
3.	1	13.	2
4.	4	14.	3
5.	3	15.	1
6.	3	16.	2
7.	3	17.	3
8.	5	18.	2
9.	1	19.	2
10.	3		

EXERCISE 11

1.	whether	9.	mail
2.	scene	10.	Your
3.	grate	11.	principle; principal
4.	counsel	12.	Steel
5.	their; their	13.	have
6.	capital	14.	hear; you're
7.	stationary	15.	too
8.	plain		

EXERCISE 12

1.	thorough	8.	accept
2.	advice	9.	dessert
3.	lose	10.	personnel
4.	Where	11.	illicit
5.	affect	12.	clothes
6.	conscious	13.	bathe
7.	proceed		

EXERCISE 13

1.	2	11.	5
2.	1	12.	3
3.	3	13.	2
4.	1	14.	2
5.	4	15.	4
6.	5	16.	1
7.	1	17.	1
8.	5	18.	5
9.	1	19.	1
10.	3	20.	2

EXERCISE 14

1.	inconveniently	9.	you're
2.	received	10.	Where
3.	OK	11.	OK
4.	psychologist	12.	beauty
5.	illegal	13.	roommate
6.	preferred	14.	shield
7.	financially	15.	stationery
8.	noisily		

EXERCISE 15

1.	psychologist	5.	I'm
2.	Ms.	6.	doctor
3.	OK	7.	Her
4.	uncle		

EXERCISE 16

1. Does aunt barbara still live in las vegas, nevada?

2. thomas jefferson lived at monticello, his home in virginia.

3. I grew up in the midwest but went to college in the east.

4. My friend darius, the crazy new yorker, lives in manhattan near the george washington bridge.

5. Anita, a professor at the university of georgia in athens, says many northerners go to school in the south.

6. in san francisco, I took a cable car to post street.

7. Whenever cousin edward eats italian food, he recalls the days he spent in milan, italy, during world war II.

EXERCISE 17

1. The republicans have many wealthy supporters in large companies such as the xerox corporation.

2. The democrats gained seats in the House, while the republicans gained seats in the Senate.

3. The main offices of the united steel workers are in Pittsburgh.

4. To lose weight, Julie took dexatrim and joined weight watchers.

5. Call the better business bureau, and see if the charitable organization is registered.

6. Anita is active in the girl scouts of america.

7. My favorite snack, chee·tos, is made by frito-lay, inc., whose national headquarters are in Dallas.

EXERCISE 18

1. would a presbyterian view religious holidays differently from a catholic?

2. if you took high school math, you should be ready for mathematics 101 in college.

3. uncle carl and aunt helga are close friends with professor rappaport, who teaches russian at a community college in my state.

4. the auto mechanic at midas told me he had learned his trade at the andrew jackson vocational school.

5. cynthia is studying computer science at the national institute of technology.

6. dr. mustafa azawi is an expert on islamic law and the koran.

7. if you join the jazz band, you'll get credit for music appreciation 201.

8. my favorite class is called latin american literature in the twentieth century; it is taught by a professor from columbia. we read the books in spanish, but classes are conducted in english.

9. the rabbi spoke of god and read in hebrew from the torah.

10. my uncle in korea took me to several buddhist temples.

62

EXERCISE 19

1.	4	11.	5
2.	2	12.	4
3.	1	13.	2
4.	1	14.	1
5.	3	15.	3
6.	4	16.	2
7.	1	17.	1
8.	1	18.	3
9.	4	19.	2
10.	2	20.	2

EXERCISE 20

1. Did you see *A Nightmare on Elm Street* when it first came out?
2. We sang "We Shall Overcome" in memory of Dr. Martin Luther King, Jr.
3. The book *A Night to Remember* is about the sinking of the Titanic.
4. My cousin, Al Morales, M.D., referred me to you, Doctor.
5. My favorite mystery by P.D. James is *A Taste for Death.*
6. Last night we watched *From Here to Eternity,* a movie about World War II.
7. When the Concorde takes off for Europe, General Stone, U.S.A.F., will be aboard.
8. *West Side Story* is loosely based on Shakespeare's *Romeo and Juliet.*

EXERCISE 21

1. our anniversary, may 28, sometimes falls on memorial day.
2. macy's is open late on monday and thursday evenings.
3. florists always look forward to February 14, valentine's day.
4. we always celebrate thanksgiving on the fourth thursday in november.
5. the coins are believed to date back to somewhere between 50 b.c. and 100 a.d.
6. the office will be closed thursday and friday because we must take the monthly inventory.
7. every thirty days, more or less, we begin a new month.
8. i can never remember if halloween is on october 30 or october 31.
9. the months that have thirty days are september, april, june, and november.
10. the employees want to take the holiday on monday or friday, which would extend their weekend to three days.

EXERCISE 22

february 6, 1991

Mr. Jacob hargreaves

Perfect cookbooks, inc.

1946 Elm ave.

Chicago, Illinois 60600

Dear mr. Hargreaves:

In november, i ordered a set of your cookbooks, which i had seen advertised in *ladies' home journal.* it is now february, and i have not received any of the books. I couldn't even use the recipes i especially wanted for christmas cookies and fruit cake!

if you cannot guarantee that i'll have the books in six weeks—no later than march 15—please return my check. I hope to use the easter cake decorating tips i read about, so i must have the books next month.

sincerely,

estelle Louis

Howe Park Bake shoppe

EXERCISE 23

stephen smith lay in bed at monroe hospital, his mother by his side. "my son," wept mrs. smith, "was shot for wearing the wrong thing, and that's all."

on wednesday, june 10, mr. smith was shot while waiting for a bus on oak street near harbor drive. he was wearing a purple scarf with his blue windbreaker. "i didn't realize," he said later, "that those were the colors of the majestic knights or that i was on the turf of the green demons."

a passerby, jacklyn michaels, told the *daily news,* "as the attackers drove off, i saw them making gang signals." ms. michaels, a medical student at leland university, immediately shouted for help and began first aid. chong dae park, a korean immigrant who had arrived in the city only the previous saturday, heard her cries and called 911 from a nearby pay phone. "please send help!" he told the dispatcher. "a man is shot near burger king on oak street."

mr. park and ms. michaels later joined stephen's mother at the hospital, where the doctor made an announcement. "i have good news," said dr. vega. "this young man will be home in time to celebrate independence day with his family on july 4!"

EXERCISE 24

1.	1	11.	1
2.	5	12.	2
3.	4	13.	2
4.	4	14.	2
5.	1	15.	1
6.	4	16.	2
7.	4	17.	3
8.	5	18.	4
9.	1	19.	4
10.	3	20.	1

EXERCISE 25

1. Dr. Williams charges $48.00 for an office visit.
2. Mark your calendar for Fri., Mar. 12th.
3. The school is almost two miles (1.7 to be exact) from our home on W. Hampshire St.
4. This station sells gas for $1.75 a gallon. I need 18.8 gallons to fill my empty tank.
5. Rev. Caldwell's notes read: "I worked on this sermon from Mon. to Fri."
6. Acme Printing, Inc., is located on Seventh St. near the U.S. Post Office.
7. The baby, named Joseph Cole, Jr., weighed 7 lbs., 3 oz., at birth.
8. As Mr. and Mrs. Fareed entered, everyone became quiet.
9. On the receipt he wrote, "$12 recd., full amt. pd."
10. Carpeting is $10.95 per sq. yd. The rm. is 10 ft. by 12 ft., so we need 120 sq. ft.

EXERCISE 26

1. "I won!" exclaimed Georgianna.
2. The fireman asked, "Do you have a smoke alarm?"
3. "Stop, thief!" shouted the enraged shopkeeper.
4. Frank wondered when the babysitter would show up.
5. How much rain has fallen in the past hour?
6. "Get out of the apartment!" ordered the tenant.
7. The instructor asked how many people had taken the test before.
8. "What a hoax!" sputtered the swindled investors.
9. Don't bananas contain a lot of potassium?
10. Where can the children be? I am so worried about them.
11. "A question we should ask ourselves before bringing a pet into the home," began the talk show host, "is whether we truly will commit ourselves to providing for its welfare."
12. Is there an emergency exit? Let's ask the landlord.
13. Good heavens! Did you expect a surprise party?
14. Would you please get it right this time? I've retyped this letter six times so far!
15. If all twenty of us contribute ten dollars to the pot, we will have $200.00 for the office party.

EXERCISE 27

1. Be sure all the dishes, glasses, and pans are clean.
2. The population of the United States in 1980 was 226,504,825.
3. We have offices in Los Angeles, California, and Dallas, Texas.
4. John, we need to get 15,000 more signatures on the petition by October 10, 1991.
5. Alesandro speaks Portuguese, Spanish, and English.
6. Soft drinks and snacks are included in the cost, Miss Wyzinski.
7. The breakfast special consists of bacon and eggs, orange or tomato juice, and freshly baked muffins.
8. OK
9. Thank you, Professor, for your help and support.
10. July 4, 1776, is a significant date in the history of the United States.

EXERCISE 28

1. While driving to San Antonio, Luis and Carmen saw three dead jackrabbits at the side of the road.
2. OK
3. He packed his bags, and he put them in the back seat of his Chevy pickup.
4. I bought the suit on sale, but I had to pay full price for the shoes.
5. OK
6. Frankly, I did not enjoy the movie very much.
7. When you go to the store, please buy me a gallon of milk.
8. We must learn to work together as a team, or we will fail.

EXERCISE 29

1. Our oldest male relative, who will be ninety-five this April, lives in Manitoba.
2. Crossing the Atlantic in a small sailboat is quite a feat, even if your name is Christopher Columbus.
3. Lee said gloomily, "We cannot afford a vacation this year."
4. OK
5. You can expect your check to arrive by Tuesday, but not sooner.
6. Jane, leaving the home in which she grew up, turned to her family and said, "This is the start of a new life for me."
7. "The more money I make," said Joe, "the more money I owe."
8. We will, of course, repair the damaged television set free of charge.

EXERCISE 30

1. 4		6. 3
2. 1		7. 4
3. 5		8. 1
4. 4		9. 2
5. 1		

EXERCISE 31

Different answers are possible. Here are some suggestions.

1. Marty's sister died of lung cancer; thus, he always urges his friends to quit smoking.
2. Your illness is very contagious; therefore, wash the thermometer well.
3. The wedding itself will be small; however, there will be a huge reception when the couple return from their honeymoon.
4. Mix all the ingredients; then, pour the batter in a cake pan.
5. Mattie has cataracts in both eyes; in addition, she is completely deaf in one ear.
6. Jack and I broke up last week; still, I have to admit that I love him.
7. In general, small cars get good gas mileage; moreover, many have front-wheel drive to assure good handling on ice and snow.
8. Courtney plans to be a lawyer; furthermore, she plans to have a family.

EXERCISE 32

1. The snow is falling steadily; it appears we're in for a blizzard.
2. Mrs. Davis is proud of her sons and daughters: Howard, the computer programmer; Janice, the engineer; Glenn, the teacher; and Belinda, the beautician.
3. The meeting is important; please be there.
4. The Pistons scored six baskets in a row; they seemed to have the court to themselves.
5. Mac will bring potato chips, onion dip, and guacamole; Judy will bring an assortment of cheeses; and Ted will bring soft drinks.
6. Damp weather is bad for people with arthritis; many such people move to Arizona because of its dry climate.
7. The sky was gloomy on the day of the funeral; it rained and rained.
8. The salesman's territory covers Rochester, Minnesota; Chicago, Illinois; and Milwaukee, Wisconsin.
9. Please call us; we need to speak with you.
10. There are many good coupons in today's paper; I plan to use every one!

EXERCISE 33

1. 4		6. 5
2. 4		7. 4
3. 3		8. 1
4. 3		9. 1
5. 4		

EXERCISE 34

1. Learn to spell the words in List I: *receive, believe, thief, neighbor,* and *weigh.*
2. Dear Representative Luhm:
3. You must return at 3:00; therefore, you have two hours to shop.
4. Important: Keep the doors locked after business hours.
5. People of all ages are welcome: toddlers, children, teens, adults, and senior citizens.

66

EXERCISE 34 (continued)

6. Dear Sir or Madam:
   In the enclosed package are five unordered items: one umbrella, two rainhats, one pair of gloves, and one folding raincoat.
7. The items you need are as follows: paper, pencils, and an eraser.
8. The members voted for the following officers: secretary, treasurer, vice-president, and sergeant-at-arms.
9. Don't show up before 9:00 because the doors will be locked.
10. Remember: The election will be held this Tuesday.

EXERCISE 35

1. Mrs. Kelly's job
2. the men's room
3. Dr. Kraus's office
4. the unions' pension plans
5. her company's benefits
6. the teachers' meeting room
7. ladies' shoes
8. my boss's personality
9. Ms. Sosa's car
10. the Sosas' landlord
11. the children's drawings
12. babies' outfits

EXERCISE 36

1. A person's worth shouldn't be measured by his or her bank balance.
2. Jackie's handwriting is terrible; her *u*'s, *v*'s, and *w*'s all look the same.
3. Can't anyone drive Mrs. Kubik to her doctor's office? She needs to see him, and I'm certain she's too weak to go alone.
4. I'll call Lynette's office as soon as the phone lines are clear.
5. Our son's teachers are working with him on his speech sounds, especially his *ing*'s and *th*'s.
6. What's the name of the new student? It's important that I know.
7. Pretzels, potato chips, cookies, and greasy hamburgers are my children's favorite foods; I can't get them to eat any vegetables.

8. We didn't know whether to believe what the three boys had told us; the boys' version of yesterday's events was quite different from the men's version.

EXERCISE 37

1. 4		11. 1	
2. 1		12. 2	
3. 2		13. 4	
4. 1		14. 5	
5. 4		15. 2	
6. 1		16. 4	
7. 1		17. 1	
8. 1		18. 2	
9. 5		19. 3	
10. 4		20. 1	

EXERCISE 38

1. Harry said, "This is the nut and bolt assembly for the latch."
2. "How do you know?" asked his assistant.
3. "Because it's labeled clearly," explained Harry.
4. The less-experienced worker asked, "How could I have missed that?"
5. Who said, "We're all in big trouble"?
6. "Weren't the Marx Brothers' old routines funny?" asked Belle.
7. "Are you ready to order?" asked the waiter.
8. The mail carrier said, "There is twelve cents postage due on this letter."
9. The theater manager shouted, "No smoking is allowed!"
10. "Isn't that an informative article?" asked the librarian.

EXERCISE 39

1. OK
2. OK
3. "On holiday weekends, drive very carefully," cautioned Paula.
4. "For all you know," said Cecile, "that could have been a burglar trying to see if anyone was at home."
5. "Let's drop the subject," pleaded Amanda. "I don't even want to think about it."
6. "Do you want another cup of coffee," offered David, "or would a glass of milk calm your nerves?"

7. OK
8. "By all means, let's see it," suggested Leopold.
9. OK
10. OK

EXERCISE 40

1. Do you remember when Mom sang "The Star-Spangled Banner" at my Little League game? I was absolutely mortified!
2. Lia asked the teacher, "Do you think I am really ready to take the GED test?"
3. "How should I know?" responded her brother. "You never tell me what's going on."
4. Did you read the article "It's a Matter of Time" in last week's *Journal*? It was fascinating.
5. Who shouted "Fire!" in the crowded theater?
6. "Lying on the beach while listening to the radio is one of my favorite summertime activities," Carlos told Gina.
7. Do you know the words to the song "Rhythm Nation" by Janet Jackson?
8. Even though the assignment required that all of us use the same title, "Trying to Change the Things We Can't," all the essays turned out quite differently.

EXERCISE 41

1. "What time is it?" asked the driver.
2. Laurie asked why we had left so early.
3. OK
4. The sign in the window said, "Sale on genuine leather coats."
5. "Hi, fellows," said Mr. Maxwell. "What's going on?"
6. OK
7. I can't stand it when my sister cracks her knuckles; she really knows how to get to me!
8. Who told Megan that she should sing "Home on the Range" at the top of her lungs?
9. "When the refrigerator door opens," explained the repairman, "the motor works harder."
10. OK
11. "Today," the coach warned his players, "will be our last full practice before the big game."
12. "Don't the pines smell terrific?" asked Daisy.
13. I'm not sure who wrote "The Moonlight Sonata."

EXERCISE 42

1.	3	11.	2
2.	4	12.	5
3.	3	13.	2
4.	4	14.	1
5.	1	15.	4
6.	4	16.	2
7.	1	17.	5
8.	3	18.	4
9.	1	19.	1
10.	1	20.	1